This Cider Still Tastes Funny!

Center Point
Large Print

Also by John Ford and available from
Center Point Large Print:

Suddenly, the Cider Didn't Taste So Good!

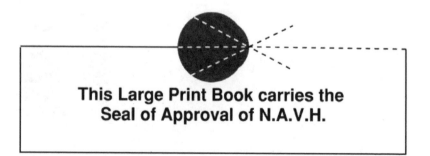

This Cider Still Tastes Funny!

Further Adventures of a Maine Game Warden

John Ford, Sr.

CENTER POINT LARGE PRINT
THORNDIKE, MAINE

This Center Point Large Print edition is published in the
year 2015 by arrangement with Islandport Press.

The text of this Large Print edition is unabridged.
In other aspects, this book may vary
from the original edition.
Printed in the United States of America
on permanent paper.
Set in 16-point Times New Roman type.

ISBN: 978-1-62899-753-8

Library of Congress Cataloging-in-Publication Data

Ford, John, 1947–
  This cider still tastes funny! : further adventures of a Maine game
warden / John Ford Sr.
  pages cm
  Summary: "A retired Maine game warden and master storyteller
recounts some of his adventures with a touch of humor"—Provided by
publisher.
  ISBN 978-1-62899-753-8 (library binding : alk. paper : large print)
  1. Game wardens—Maine—Waldo County—Anecdotes.
     2. Game protection—Maine—Waldo County—Anecdotes.
     3. Ford, John, 1947– I. Title.
SK403.F673 2015
639.909741′52—dc23
                                                    2015028918

I would like to dedicate this book to the loves of my life—my wife, Judith, and my son, John Jr.

For over twenty years they were subjected to many interruptions and stresses on their own lives—from folks calling at all hours of the day and night with complaints that required my immediate presence.

Their personal sacrifices over the years—putting up with a dad, who, more often than not, was never home when they needed or wanted him the most—is commendable in every way.

It was their undying support and thorough understanding of my profession throughout the years that allowed my career to become the one that it was. I owe them much and I love them dearly!

This Cider Still Tastes Funny!

Table of Contents

Prologue: The Way It Was

I began my career as a game warden on September 20, 1970. In doing so, I followed in the footsteps of family members who also served for years in law enforcement. My grandfather Leland Ford was a Maine state trooper, my father, Velmore Ford was a part-time deputy for the York County Sheriff's Office, and my step-father, Warden Vernon Walker, patrolled the Sanford-Springvale area for twenty-three years. And Mother, Ethelind Walker, spent hours upon hours helping rehabilitate wildlife for the Department of Fish and Game. As a result, as I mentioned in my first book, *Suddenly, the Cider Didn't Taste So Good*, working in law enforcement was a childhood dream of mine as I grew up in the Sanford, Maine, area.

When I finally became a game warden in 1970, it truly was a dream come true, and the following twenty years I spent as a game warden did nothing to change that feeling.

However, as my career wound down in the late 1980s, the times and the job were rapidly changing. There is no question everything was much different then it is today.

On my first official day of work, I was issued a used cruiser—a sedan from a warden who was terminally ill and ready to retire. I was also provided with several new uniforms, law books, a couple of badges, a brass compass, a used .38 caliber Smith and Wesson handgun, a gun belt, a sleeping bag, a flashlight, and a summons book. These were the items given to new recruits and were considered everything we would need to perform our official duties.

That first day I was greeted by Warden Supervisor Charles Allen and Inspector Lee Downs at the Burnham Warden's Camp (supervisor is the equivalent in rank to today's lieutenant, and inspector the equivalent in rank to today's sergeant).

The two men showed me how to complete required paperwork, gave me a tour of the district, and then left. If I made it through my probationary period, I would need to attend the next wardens' school, which ran from February through April, at the University of Maine. I was mostly on my own, except when my partner, Warden Norman Gilbert from Hartland, was able to join me to show me the ropes and teach me the area.

And that is how things were done back then. It was kind of an on-the-job training process, much different than the highly structured training required today.

But that's not all that has changed. When I started, snowmobiling, for example, was just starting to increase in popularity as a winter activity. And back then, a machine capable of traveling more than 40 mph was considered a real screamer—a far cry from what we see today. Had anyone said back then that someday we'd unpack a machine from its crate that was guaranteed to travel upward of 100 mph or more, I'd have accused them of smoking some of that "wacky-tobacky" I sometimes found growing in the woods of Thorndike, Maine.

Unfortunately, such speeds are exactly what we see these days. I say *unfortunately* because it's the unfortunate game warden who must respond to a scene where some daredevil has attempted to sail through the woods on a four-foot-wide trail, full of bumps and hidden obstacles, at speeds that even Evel Knievel would have considered too dangerous. Yup, today's warden may be "blessed" with the gruesome task of picking up body parts and notifying the next of kin that Junior won't be coming home for supper ever again.

In 1970, witnessing a bald eagle soaring over-head was a rarity. Man's own neglect and use of pesticides and other chemicals nearly caused the extinction of our national bird. Today, eagles once again flourish in our skies, thanks to scientific research, good protection, and the recognition that these pesticides did more harm than good.

In 1970, the thought of wild turkeys roaming

our countryside was unheard of; turkey buzzards were native only to states far south of ours. Today, turkeys have become a nuisance of sorts. Right here in Waldo County, we introduced thirty-two birds on farmland in the town of Waldo in 1984. Now there are turkeys throughout all of central Maine and beyond as a result of this small flock of birds, and a few others. The turkey program was a huge success—too much so, in the eyes of some.

The State of Maine was seriously debating whether or not we had coyotes roaming our woodlands in 1970. Biologists insisted these wild creatures were "coy-dogs" and not coyotes. In 1973, I had my first official encounter with one of these critters when a large male coyote was struck and killed by an automobile on a back road in south Unity. The mere sight of the critter made headlines in the local papers. Today, there isn't a single section of this state that hasn't been invaded by these unwanted predators.

In 1970, the idea of a legal moose hunt was considered crazy talk. As a matter of fact, anyone caught shooting a moose was considered to have committed the cardinal poaching sin according to Fish and Game statutes. To be found guilty of a "moose murder" was a major crime, punishable by severe penalties.

In the early years of my career, night-hunting, despite being illegal, was a way of life for many folks within my district. For example, several residents in the town of Burnham where I'd taken up residency claimed that in order to be considered a bona fide resident of the town, a person must have been convicted of night-hunting at least once.

Indeed, for the first few years I served as a warden, Burnham definitely held the reputation as being the top deer-poaching area of central Maine (although the neighboring town of Troy certainly came in a close second). The penalty for night-hunting was a mere $200 fine, and required no jail time unless unusual circumstances warranted such a drastic measure. Violators were even allowed to keep their firearms and the equipment they used to commit this illegal act. In a few instances, individuals convicted of night-hunting were caught as repeat offenders within a few nights of being apprehended the first time.

Today, penalties are much more severe for night-hunting and deer-poaching. There is an automatic jail sentence of three days for the first offense, and more for the second. Any equipment used in committing the act is seized and forfeited to the State of Maine, to be sold later at a public auction. The fine was initially increased from $200 to $500, and although the increased fine helped for a brief period of time, it didn't seem to cut down on the activity. Consequently, the fine was raised to $1,000 for the first offense and more for the second.

It was quite a change from my first few years when I spent night after night pursuing the intentional violator. While the increased penalties have helped reduce poaching, they have also increased the danger posed to a warden who is attempting to make an arrest out on some back road in the middle of the night.

On another positive note a new law that required hunters to wear blaze orange has helped reduce hunting accidents.

In 1970, we experienced an abundance of partridge, woodcock, coon, rabbits, bobcat, fisher, fox, and beaver roaming in our backyards. I still recall many a summer night, sitting outside and listening to the sounds of a whip-poor-will in a nearby field. It's been several years since I've heard their shrill call. It appears yet another species has disappeared from our region.

The weather also seems to have changed compared to back in the 1970s. If the weatherman forecast a blizzard back in those days, we usually got clobbered with a whopping twelve to twenty inches of snow—not the four inches we often get today which is often labeled "the storm of the century" by the news media. There's little doubt our climatic conditions have changed, but if one took the time to review the past ages, they'd find the weather has always fluctuated. It seems to run in cycles.

I recall a snowstorm in the early 1970s when

we got twenty-seven inches of snow in a two-day period. Thank God my neighbor had a bucket loader to scoop out my driveway, or I'd still be shoveling!

In 1970, a fisherman could carry a small fishing-law pamphlet that he could quickly read and understand. Today that same fisherman would need a briefcase to carry the damn thing around, and he would need to be accompanied by two Philadelphia lawyers and a Boston judge to interpret it. Trying to abide by the new regulations can be a chore. For example, trying to understand where you're allowed to use what kind of bait, and when, or what the limits and sizes of fish are from one area of the state to the next has created mass confusion. More than one person has unintentionally fallen victim to a mistaken interpretation of one of these laws.

The opening day of deer season in the 1970s was a highly anticipated event. Hunters largely had the freedom to hunt wherever they desired without being called out for trespassing. Posted property was not common in the region, as neighbors allowed neighbors to go wherever they wished in pursuit of game. Most of my district was invaded by hunters, residents, and non-residents alike (and, as a result, I, as warden, always found some type of shady activity to investigate and occupy my time). Roads were often lined with parked cars, and hunters scurried from one patch of woods to another. It was a special time. It appears that the old family tradition of fathers and their sons or daughters enjoying a day's hunt together is starting to fade.

No longer are the roadsides lined with the parked cars of hunters. The amount of open land for hunters has diminished. Places that were once prime hunting areas are now posted and restricted.

In 1970, had anyone told me that I'd be required to go out into the field searching for milfoil, I'd have thought I was looking for something to cover a salad dish in order to keep it fresh.

If anyone had said back then that one day I'd be able to travel freely over the snow on a trail system that expands from one end of the state to the other, I wouldn't have believed it—especially if they'd told me I could do so at 100 mph.

In those early days of my career, it was rare to hear about a violent crime in our state. And when such an event did occur, it was a major topic of discussion for days. Today, the armed robberies, rapes, murders, and other violent crimes so common in other states seem to be increasingly common right here in our own backyards.

Yup, times have changed. Some changes are for the best, and some are not. I personally enjoyed the excitement and anxiety of those earlier days.

I considered my times on duty as though I was going to the movies and knew an adventure was sure to follow. I didn't know if it would be a wildlife adventure, a crime-scene investigation, a search-and-rescue mission, or a high-speed chase—but I knew I was in for an adventure!

As I have mentioned before, the best advice I ever received was from my mentor, Game Warden Vernon Walker, who told me to keep a diary. I did, and that has allowed me to remember my days as a game warden during what I consider to be the best of times for the warden service. And as I was set to retire in 1990, I was also convinced that times had changed too much for me to continue, although I was confident those wardens who followed in my footsteps would enjoy their careers, although different, just as much as I did.

Well, maybe almost as much as I did.

I Gotta Go!

Late one October evening in 1971, I found myself working in the St. Albans, Maine, area with veteran partner, Warden Norman Gilbert. We'd just snuggled into place to patiently wait for a night-hunter to come along when suddenly a pickup truck slowly drove up to the edge of the field we were watching and came to a stop. The passengers began scouting the entire area from inside the truck with a huge, bright, handheld spotlight. It was obvious they were searching for the yellow eyes of a hypnotized deer, blinded by the bright beam of light being cast into its face. Not finding any deer in this field, the men in the truck slowly proceeded to the next. We promptly pulled in behind the truck, following quietly with our lights off.

Once again, the beam of light was cast from inside their vehicle, illuminating the entire area. Little did they know we were situated just a few feet behind them. My heart was pounding with excitement, wondering whether or not these bandits were going to be cooperative, or if we'd soon be involved in a high-speed chase. Initiating the signal lights and the headlights in our cruiser, we signaled for them to pull over. Instead, they shot off down the highway and away we went. It was going to be a chase!

Norman remained glued to their back bumper like a wart on a toad's tail. Realizing they weren't about to get away, they suddenly pulled over to the side of the road, coming to a sudden and rather abrupt stop, whereby we damn near mowed them down like a big blade of grass. This was a smart move on their part, seeing that Norman was in a ramming mood, and doubtless wouldn't have hesitated to exercise the need if he felt it was warranted.

I exited my side of the cruiser at a dead run, heading straight for the passenger's side of the vehicle as Norman ran to the driver's side. Yanking the passenger's door open, I saw that he was frozen in place. He had a .30-06 rifle between his legs and a plug-in spotlight sprawled across his lap. There was no question what they were up to. I quickly secured the rifle before someone got hurt, and at the same time Norman informed the two men they were under arrest for night-hunting.

The clip and shells for the firearm were not with the weapon. In order to prove our case, we needed all of the items used to commit the crime, including the ammo that would fit the gun they possessed.

"Okay, fellas, where are the shells for this rifle?" I asked.

"There ain't any!" the passenger responded. "We forgot to bring them with us."

I knew better, and so did he. He was about as nervous and uncomfortable as a kid about ready to have a tooth yanked from his mouth by a mean old dentist. Instructing him to please step out of the vehicle so I could conduct a search for the missing shells, he uneasily honored the request. As he climbed out of the truck I was in awe at his size. He appeared to be close to seven feet tall and was built like a professional wrestler. His neck alone was bigger than my waist. (You have to realize this was in my younger years, before age caught up with my midsection.)

As he stepped out of the truck, he anxiously stated, "I've got to go to the bathroom!"

"Not until I conduct my search for the missing clip and shells," I snapped as I started a methodical search in and around the seat of the vehicle, hunting for the missing items.

"I've got to go—and I've got to go *now!*" he sputtered.

"I'll let you go in a minute, sir, just as soon as I'm finished here," I said.

"I don't think I can wait much longer." By now he was pleading.

I figured he might possibly have the clip and shells in his possession and was merely looking for a means to get rid of them. A bathroom call would be the perfect opportunity to accomplish such a feat. I kept a watchful eye on him as I continued searching for the missing items. Reaching far up beneath the seat of the truck, I finally found the metal clip and shells that fit the rifle they had with them. Now we had the evidence we needed to make our case.

Turning back to my prisoner, who by now was extremely silent, I said, "Okay, my friend, you can go to the bathroom now if you want."

Disgustedly he grumbled, "I don't have to now!"

He'd gone in his pants. The odor of human feces was quite evident as I went to search him for more evidence. By no means was this a very pleasant situation. It was all I could do not to gag as I frisked him, looking for more shells and evidence.

Managing to catch Norman's attention, I whispered, "We've got a problem here, Norm!"

"What's that?" Norman inquired.

Speaking as softly as I could, I said, "This guy has shit himself!"

Norman said drily, "That's no problem as I see it. I'll just take the driver to jail in my cruiser and you can ride with him in their truck. That way he won't smell up my cruiser!"

"What about me? I'll have to smell it all the way," I bitterly complained.

With that smirk that only Norman possessed, he said, "John, John, John . . . I heard him ask you several times to go to the bathroom and you denied him, so really, who caused this dilemma? It looks to me as if it's more your problem than mine." The old goat grinned.

"I suggest you roll the window down and hopefully the fresh air will make your trip to the county lockup a little more enjoyable."

All Aboard

"John, this is Mr. Jones, from the town of Thorndike." I could hear the man's anger over the phone. "I want to complain about that gawd-damned train that comes up through here daily, hauling grain to Burnham. Them sons of bitches are shooting deer from it whenever there's one standing within range."

"How do you know that's what they're doing?" I asked.

"Damn it all to hell! They stopped just below my place late yesterday afternoon and fired at a big doe, right from the caboose," he said. "The deer didn't fall, so they never bothered to see if they'd wounded her or not! I don't know if there's much you can do about it, but I just wanted you to know it's happening."

"Okay, Mr. Jones, I'll look into it," I promised, silently wondering what approach I'd take. The chances of seeing anyone shooting from the train were remote at best.

For the next few days I kept thinking about how best to handle this complaint. I shared Mr. Jones's concerns during a conversation with a friend who also lived along the tracks.

"Funny you should mention it, John. The other day I heard shots down below my house," he said. "Within minutes, the train slowly poked its way past our place as it headed toward Thorndike. Now that I think about it, there might be some truth to what Mr. Jones is telling you."

Now, with two different reports of railroad crewmen possibly hunting from the train, my attention was focused on some sort of law enforcement action, if nothing more than to let them know I'd heard about their illegal activities. Having been on the job for just a few short weeks, I didn't want folks thinking I was ignoring their complaints.

I spent the next couple of days scanning the route of the Belfast & Moosehead Lake train as it traveled from Belfast to Burnham. The daily routine usually called for a quick stop in Thorndike before they continued on to Burnham Junction. I decided my best chance of capturing these banditos, if in fact they were violating the law, would be to make a sudden appearance on the train, hoping to find a loaded rifle or shotgun.

My plan called for a quick trip to Unity, where I could hide in the bushes along the railroad tracks outside of town. The train, which never traveled very fast to begin with, would slow down as it approached the crossings coming onto Depot Street in Unity. As it slowed, I intended to exit the bushes and scale the steps leading up into the caboose. I'd barge through the door and hopefully find the loaded firearm, if it existed. At the very least, I'd alert those involved that I was wise to their actions and was following up on a complaint.

Late in the afternoon, I watched the train as it pulled into the Thorndike yard. From off in the distance I counted the number of cars behind the engine, so I'd know exactly where the caboose was in relation to the rest of the train. There were eleven freight cars being towed by the large engine, followed by the caboose.

I quickly headed off to Unity, pulling in behind the local hardware store where I exited my cruiser. Running as fast as I could, I shot down the railroad tracks to a secluded area. The wait was on. Before long I heard the squealing of the huge metal wheels grinding on the rickety old tracks as the train slowly proceeded my way. My heart began pounding with excitement as I anticipated what the next few minutes might bring.

The noise grew louder and louder as the big metal monster gradually came into view. Ducking down into the bushes for cover, I anxiously waited for it to pass within four feet of where I was hiding. There was the engine—*one, two, three, four, five*—I counted the cars as they rock-and-rolled past me. *Eight, nine, ten* . . . It was time to go. I shot out of the bushes and stood alongside the moving train, anxiously waiting for that caboose to come into view. I knew I only had one shot at it, and hoped I was making the right move.

I felt as though I was in an old Western cowboy show where the good guy hops onto a moving train, hoping to rescue a damsel in distress—the difference being that my purpose was to send a message, if nothing else.

I could see the steps at the front of the caboose approaching. My heart raced as I anticipated making the flying leap up onto the moving train. It couldn't have worked out any better. I shot out of the bushes and grabbed onto the railing leading onto the platform of the moving caboose. Poor old Charlie, a member of the crew, was standing on the other side of the platform as I scaled it. I scared the ever-living bejeezus out of him as I burst through the door of the caboose, hoping to find the loaded weapon I figured would be in plain sight.

The crewmen on board were all seated around a small table, playing cards. I ordered them to stop the train as I conducted my search for the firearm I hoped to find. They notified the engineer to shut down operations, which he did. The sudden and rather abrupt stop caused me to fall over a bag of grain lying on the floor. There I lay, sprawled out on the floor, looking up into the shocked faces of the startled crew. Springing back to my feet, I informed them of my reason for being there.

"Ain't got no gun here," one of the crewmen said. Then, after a brief pause, he added, "Well, there is an old shotgun in the closet." He opened the door and removed the beat-up old weapon, which wasn't loaded.

Advising them of the complaints I'd received of shots being fired from the moving train, I searched the small caboose for any more weapons. Finding none, I politely thanked them for their excellent cooperation and departed the ironclad monster just as quickly as I'd entered it. I was quite sure that by now they knew I was aware of any illegal activity they might be involved in, and happily, I never received another complaint from those living along the rails.

The crazy antics of the new warden in town quickly circulated throughout the countryside. Over the next few days, I was sarcastically asked by several people, "Boarded any trains lately, John?"

A few years later, one of the crew members who had been in the caboose that day recalled the event. "You really messed up, John! The firearm you were looking for was up in the engine and not in the caboose," he said, laughing. "You had the wrong end of the train!"

Free Willy

It was another wet, windy, and miserable fall night, as a coastal storm was pounding our part of the country. The wind was blowing up a gale, and it was raining like a cow peeing on a flat rock. The weather was so horrid that Bill Pidgeon, my working partner, and I decided to give ourselves a night off from the normal routine.

The conditions were almost identical to those of a few nights before, when I'd left poor Bill sitting on a stone wall in Troy as I chased after a night-hunter. Bill had been huddled in his rain gear down by the roadside, where he could get a better view of any activity occurring as vehicles passed by our location. If anything happened, the plan called for me to drive over and pick him up so we could pursue the offenders together.

Unfortunately, the plan didn't work out as well as it should have. A slow-moving vehicle passed by our location, illegally illuminating the entire area as it crept on past us. I pulled down to the roadside, waiting for Bill to jump in, but there was no Bill. The offending vehicle was getting farther and farther away; I either had to make my move right then or let them go. We had spent way too many hours sitting night after night, waiting for something like this to happen, to simply let an offender drive off into the darkness, so I made a command decision to pursue the vehicle before it was too late to legally say I had kept a continuous watch of their actions. Bill later told me that he'd just been reaching for my door handle when I shot away from him to make the stop.

Needless to say, the offender was, in fact, night-hunting, evidenced by the loaded rifle perched alongside him. He was arrested, which meant I had to drive to Belfast some thirty miles away in order to book him into the county jail, leaving poor Bill on his own, cold and without a vehicle, stuck outside in the pouring rain.

When I got back and picked up Bill by the roadside, he would hardly speak to me. He was shivering and shaking, frozen to the bone. I tried my best to advise him of how I had contacted wardens Doug Tibbetts and my old working partner, Norman Gilbert, asking them to come to Bill's aid, but they had refused. Norman didn't like the fact that Bill had been teasing him recently, so he'd said to Doug, "To hell with him—let him sit there! It'll do him good." And that's what they did.

So now, a few nights after the incident, Bill was still irate at being left out in the cold. He obviously felt that another rainy night would only revive bad memories of that situation.

"Let's stay in and enjoy a night off," he said.

I actually was quite excited about spending a

night at home with my new bride for a change. Little did I know how short-lived the celebration would be.

At about 8:30 p.m., the phone rang. "Hello," I said.

"John, this is Gary over on Route 9 in Troy. Some son of a gun just fired two shots in the field beside my house. They seem to be doing it all the time lately," he griped.

"You're kidding me," I grumbled. "Who to hell would be out night-hunting on a night like this?"

"Damned if I know," Gary said, "but I'm getting some damn tired of it!"

"Okay," I said reluctantly. "I'll be out shortly."

I was quite distraught about having to go out, especially in these raw conditions. I was seriously considering just saying to hell with it, when the phone rang again.

"Hi, John," said Kate, an elderly lady living in the same neighborhood. "I just had someone stop in front of my house, lighting up my field, and they fired a shot. You asked me to call if I ever heard anything."

"I'm heading your way," I said. By now, it was obvious I couldn't just ignore what was happening. Like it or not, I had to haul my sorry tail outside and respond to the damn night-hunting complaints.

The rain was coming down in sheets with

occasional flashes of lightning, and the wind blowing a gale as I headed for Troy, hoping to locate the culprits causing all the commotion. To say I doubted I'd catch anyone was an understatement if ever there was one.

Eventually, I found myself parked in a secluded field off Barker Road in Troy, and the wait began. I was tucked in behind a small island of trees and bushes situated in the middle of the field, a perfect place to hide. I decided not to drape my parachute over the front of my car—my usual practice, designed to prevent a bright light from reflecting off the chrome or glass and giving away my presence. Big mistake.

After only a few minutes I observed the glare of headlights slowly approaching from the north. As the vehicle came into view it suddenly pulled up to the field entrance and began illuminating the area around me. My heart started pounding as the adrenaline rushed through my veins. I couldn't help but think this was way too easy, considering the countless hours and the many previous nights I'd spent out in the dark, waiting for something to happen.

As the light circled around the field and lit up the woods, much to my surprise I saw a small spike-horn buck, grazing in the wet grass just a few yards away. I saw his head lift up as he stared directly into the beam of light. Suddenly, *ka-pow!* *ka-pow!* Two rifle shots rang out as the deer turned and tried to run. The shots hit their mark, and the critter fell dead a few feet from where I was hiding.

My heart was really racing now in anticipation of what would happen next. One thing was for sure: I was about to become quite busy.

A beam of light, bobbing up and down, quickly raced toward the dead animal. Someone was out on foot headed my way, while the vehicle remained parked, adjacent to the field. As the person came closer, suddenly they spotted the reflection from the front end of my cruiser.

"It's the #$@%*& game wardens! Get the hell out of here," a man yelled as he sprinted down across the field and into the thick woods like a rabbit being chased by a hungry fox.

Making a split-second decision, I chose to pursue the vehicle, in hopes of retrieving the firearm used in this crime. As I spun out of the field in pursuit of the car, immediately it turned into a chase. The dirt road was extremely wet and slippery as we shot down over it at breakneck speeds, slipping and sliding around every corner.

Once I was on the back bumper of the offending vehicle, the driver pulled over to the side of the road and quickly gave up. It probably was a damn good thing he did, because I was known for ramming those who failed to stop, and the thought was definitely on my mind to end this chase sooner rather than later!

The lone operator, Willy, was shaking in his boots as I obtained his identity.

"What the hell are you stopping me for?" he bluntly inquired.

I said, "Well, Willy, I guess I'd kinda like to know who was with you when you just shot that deer back up the road."

"I don't know anything about any damned old deer," he replied as I searched the vehicle for a firearm and shells that I couldn't seem to find.

Obviously, these items were with whoever had run off into the woods. Oh well, I'd had a fifty-fifty chance of being right.

I quickly arrested Willy and took him back to where the dead deer was still lying in the field. I notified the barracks of my situation, requesting assistance in hopes of locating the other culprit and securing the scene.

"You guys ought to be proud of this one," I remarked as my headlights lit up the carcass of the little spike-horn buck.

"Oh, for cripe's sake!" Willy said sarcastically. "Someone has shot a deer!" He acted as though he didn't have a clue as to what had transpired in the field. He was clearly well versed in playing the part of a real dummy. Willy recognized that he was the only one being charged with a crime, and more than likely his buddy had gotten away. I charged Willy with the night-hunting offense, based on what I'd witnessed. There was absolutely no doubt in my mind that he was definitely a player in the crime.

It wasn't long before Supervisor Nash, Inspector Downs, and my working partner, Bill, showed up to assist me. The rain was coming down in buckets as the wind steadily howled.

"I thought you were taking the night off!" Bill grumbled. I could sense he was a little put out to think I was out working instead. I had to convince him it wasn't by choice that I found myself floundering around in this rainstorm.

Whoever had fled the scene would surely be wet and cold by the time they reached their destination. I only hoped they were as miserable as possible, and scared to death that I might be right behind them.

Back in those days, we didn't have trained tracking dogs or any of the other sophisticated means of hunting people down that are available in today's line of police work. In addition, the heavy rainfall made it doubtful that any means of tracking would have worked that night. Simply put, Willy's compadre was more than likely home-free.

Willy, however, was a different story. He saw his car being towed off by a local wrecker even as he received an all-expense-paid trip in wrist restraints to the Waldo County Crowbar Hotel, with me acting as his chauffeur.

We became well acquainted with each other on

the long ride south. I actually kind of admired the guy. He obviously knew he'd been in the wrong place at the wrong time, but his loyalty to a buddy wasn't about to be compromised. He'd decided to accept whatever punishment was coming to him and let the rest of it play out later on in the courts.

This was a smart move on Willy's part. During the trial a few weeks later, Willy was completely exonerated of all charges against him when his attorney detected a discrepancy in the court paperwork alleging the complaint. This so-called technicality was the first time I found myself seriously questioning just how great our judicial system truly is—it wouldn't be the last. During my career, I have witnessed many travesties of justice in cases I've worked, but overall, I guess these are the rules and regulations that make our country great.

Like it or not, I'd done my job to the best of my ability; now it was up to the courts and the prosecutors to do theirs. The legal system's checks and balances were in order, as they should have been.

Time has a way of eventually revealing secrets from the past, however. Eventually, I discovered who was with Willy that wet and windy night. From what I heard, the man did, in fact, have a miserable hike back to his house. He was on a dead run for nearly a mile, directly through the woods. Supposedly he was looking over his shoulder for the next several days, expecting me to knock on his door with an arrest warrant in hand.

The boys decided this was too close a call for them, and they vowed to never go night-hunting again. They didn't give up poaching, though; instead, they just decided it would be safer and easier to illegally shoot a deer during the daytime rather than chance it during the dark of night.

Modern-Day Robin Hood

While I was a new warden recruit traveling throughout the district, attempting to learn the area and its people, folks often asked, "Have you met Grover yet?"

"Who to hell is Grover?" I inquired.

Most everybody was quick to explain that Grover was an alleged notorious poacher with a reputation for being a real bad character—someone who required the use of extreme caution when approaching either him or his cronies. Although these comments were strictly rumors, it seemed to be a topic of conversation that came up with just about everybody I met.

They labeled Grover as an intimidating and ruthless poacher, operating around the area with an attitude of total defiance regarding any of the fish and wildlife rules. His previous actions and reputation had obviously instilled a real sense of fear into many of these folks. On more than one occasion I was strongly advised: "John, if you attempt to stop Grover or any of his gang, don't you dare turn your back on them! They'd just as soon shoot you as not!"

These words of caution instilled a personal concern in my mind, seeing as how I was just beginning my professional career in an area already noted for its violence against the local warden. This was especially true after some local thugs had shot the windows out of the warden's camp where my predecessor and his family had been living, committing this dastardly act as the young warden's wife and infant daughter lay huddled together on the floor of the small camp, fearing for their lives.

With this information on my mind, I asked several police agencies around the area if any of them were aware of this character named Grover. Not surprisingly, they were; they, too, issued the same warnings and cautions that I got from the public.

Most of Grover's associates had highly questionable reputations of their own. The main culprits seemed to hail from the Vassalboro, Waterville, and Winslow areas of central Maine. All of them had experienced more than their fair share of run-ins with the local law enforcement agencies, whether it was the local police, other wardens, sheriff's deputies, or the State Police. Every department seemed to know them well. Whenever a major crime occurred locally, their names always seemed to rise to the top of the suspect list.

This supposed gang of outlaws consisted of Grover, the leader, and members Dickey, Bobby, Moe, and Mavel, among others. The hunting season was the most popular time of the year for the gang to congregate, night after night, always as a team. During this time, Grover's associates were joined by a group of out-of-staters who themselves were not the most law-abiding of citizens. According to the rumor mill, this alleged poaching ring supposedly killed more than a hundred deer each year. These illegally killed animals were reportedly sold, bartered, or given away to friends and other associates throughout the central Maine area. Some folks actually viewed Grover as a modern-day Robin Hood of sorts, "stealing from the State and giving to the poor."

Without fail during my travels I would come across many a humble citizen who wouldn't dare report the illegal activities occurring in their neighborhoods by any of this gang, fearing retaliation. Simply being labeled a snitch by Grover and the gang instilled enough fear into people to cause them to look the other way. Obviously folks felt it would be impossible to prevent the gang's illegal hunting practices.

More than once I heard folks telling area wardens, "The word around here is that you fellows are afraid of them yourselves!" I desperately tried to assure them that I'd taken an oath to uphold and enforce the laws of our state. I wasn't about to differentiate between Grover and any other citizen who violated those rules. "He may have a bad reputation and he may have created a real sense of fear for many of you, but I promise you, I will deal with those situations when they arise," I said earnestly.

Silently, I prayed that when and if the time came, it would turn out for the best. I actually found myself dreading the time when I might meet up with this group, especially out on some back road in the middle of the night, knowing just how much they despised the profession I had chosen. I also knew that showing even the slightest indication that I was afraid or intimidated would be the worst thing I could ever do. I'd have to force myself to deal with the matter whenever it happened in the same way that I'd treat anyone else under the same circumstances. The level of respect they'd get from me would be entirely up to them.

Grover's occupations and interests varied. Besides hunting and fishing, he was quite active in other areas. During the off-season from hunting—if he ever acknowledged such a time— he served as a bouncer at a couple of sleazy bars located in and around the Waterville-Winslow area. During the day, he worked by himself as a woodcutter. Unlike most woods operators today, Grover utilized a team of work horses to do the heavy work, harvesting wood the old-fashioned way rather than using the modern technology of a skidder. The manual labor of working in the woods by hand, day after day, added sheer muscle to his already large six-foot frame. His extremely deep and intimidating voice was in and of itself an attention-getter! I knew it was only a matter of time before our paths would cross, either professionally or during a general conversation somewhere. I was anxious about meeting this supposed modern-day Robin Hood. I only hoped we could establish a form of mutual respect and rapport between us that would set the ground rules for years to come.

Occasionally we did meet as we were sailing along the highway in opposite directions. We always gave each other the evil eye as we passed. I'd offer Grover a friendly wave, and Grover returned the salute, although I couldn't quite tell if he was using all five of his fingers or just one. Nonetheless, as of yet we hadn't experienced that face-to-face confrontation that I knew was inevitable.

From what I'd determined, Grover's attitude toward killing deer was simple: He felt that taking a few every now and then and giving them to the poor was nothing more than robbing from the State to assist those who needed a little help. This theory may have sounded good in principle, but for the most part, the facts didn't seem to back up his so-called philosophy.

Grover supposedly had a favorite saying whenever he flashed a blinding light off into a dark field in the middle of the night: "If it's brown, it's down!"—meaning that if the wild critter spotted underneath the bright light was brown, the loud crack of a rifle shot would more than likely claim it as his possession.

In the early fall of 1970 I had my first encounter with the old boy. It happened strictly by chance, during a stop at a local garage in Unity. I was in the process of making another one of my many emergency runs to this establishment after poking a large hole in the muffler of my cruiser, seriously damaging the oil plug. (I often found myself cruising down some old back road that I had no business being on as I attempted to learn my new patrol area, resulting in a lot of car repairs.)

John Hubbard, the owner of the little garage who bailed me out of many of my mechanical catastrophes, anticipated my many impromptu visits. In a sense, it was job security; I was noted for keeping his business afloat. John was quite adamant in stating that whenever I needed his services, I should simply pull into the station— no appointment required. I was given top priority.

John and his wife Thelma operated the small business as a team. They had taken me under their wing like a little duckling from the very first day I'd arrived in town, and appeared to enjoy having me around. Almost daily I'd swing by to have some sort of work done on my cruiser, the inevitable consequence of trying to reach places even God hadn't visited for years on end. I operated under the warped philosophy of nickel-and-diming my State-issued cruiser to death. Occasionally, I'd throw in a quarter or fifty-cent piece after trying to access one of those remote areas I was too damned lazy to walk to.

On this particular day as I entered the garage, I noticed a large-framed man standing in the bay. He was quite loudly doing all the talking, with John and Thelma doing all the listening. The conversation consisted of normal chitchat while John appeared to be busy doing some repair work on the old blue GMC pickup truck hoisted high on the lift. I immediately recognized the truck as Grover's, and saw that it was nearly as dented and banged-up as my cruiser. Both vehicles were completely caked in a heavy layer of dried mud, had a large amount of dead grass and brush hanging from the undercarriage, and were scratched and dented from one end to the other. It was difficult to say whose wagon was torn up the most, but I guess Grover's looked a little rougher than mine. It was quite apparent that we both had been traveling in similar territories.

As I entered the garage, Grover quickly stared in my direction. When he saw it was me, he immediately ended the conversation. There was no smile on his face, but instead, a sort of irritated look of sheer defiance.

John said, "Grover, this is John Ford, our new game warden. Have you met him yet?"

I could tell just from the devious smirk on John's face that he was thoroughly enjoying this moment. John liked watching someone squirm during a time of stress or just before a confrontation of sorts. Now standing before him was the area's most notorious bad guy and the lawman who would one day be confronting him.

The introduction was a bit awkward for both of us, but I slowly walked over to Grover, offering to shake his hand. With a forced and admittedly somewhat nervous grin of my own, I said, "I certainly have heard a lot about you, Grover. I'm some damn glad to finally be meeting you."

"I'll bet you've heard a lot!" Grover said with a loud laugh. "You don't want to believe everything you hear, you know," he said.

"I don't," I replied. "Only time will separate the truth from the rumors."

Grover had a distinctly deep voice that could be heard for miles around, especially when he made what he considered an important statement, followed by a wisecrack at the end. Then he'd chuckle loudly to himself, proud for having made his point and wanting those around him to have heard it.

With the ice finally broken, we soon began talking about the many deer showing up in the area. It didn't take long before he voiced his total disgust with the Fish and Game Department's management practices, and the department as a whole. Grover appeared to be quite knowledgeable regarding the condition of the deer and moose within our area, but from what I was hearing, he should have been.

"People tell me that in order to be a good game warden, you have to have been a poacher yourself! That's what they tell me!" he said loudly, snickering. He obviously was seeking approval from John and Thelma, who by now were thoroughly enjoying every moment of our conversation.

"Oh, I don't know about that, Grover. I suppose it wouldn't hurt to have had a little inside track and experience, but it's not a prerequisite for the job by any means," I said, chuckling right back. "Perhaps someday we can sit down over a cup of coffee and share our views. I'd be quite interested in hearing yours," I said.

"Sounds good to me," Grover replied.

By now whatever tension had been evident was long gone, much to the disgruntlement of John, who wanted to continue stirring the pot in the worst way. Our first meeting had been far more cordial and reasonable than what I had expected. Truthfully speaking, I actually kind of enjoyed it. I left the garage that day feeling that perhaps Grover might not be the most honest of individuals around, but he wasn't as dangerous as he'd been portrayed—at least, not in my mind. I certainly didn't get the impression that he'd put a bullet in my head if I was to turn my back on him, as I'd been led to believe. I think his reputation had been highly exaggerated.

I actually found myself liking the man, even though it was quite evident we shared different philosophies regarding fish and wildlife rules. I hoped that we would actually sit down for a little one-on-one conversation someday—a chance to share our thoughts and to become better acquainted with each other. Grover's thorough knowledge of the outdoors was quite intriguing, to say the least. At least now I'd be able to honestly say to those folks who constantly asked if I'd met Grover, "Yup, I have! And I'm sure from what I've seen, we'll be meeting again!" And we would.

With our initial meeting finally behind us, the very next time I met Grover on the road, his wave seemed to be a little more enthusiastic and genuine. I actually think that from that day on it included a little hint of a smile—and all five of his fingers rather than just one.

What's in a Name?

Have you ever had someone try to impress you by dropping the name of someone you both might know? Certain individuals do this in hopes of persuading you that they have many friends in high places of power or authority.

I often observed this trait during my career, especially if I was in the process of bringing someone to task for a violation. This subtle name dropping usually involved a highfalutin politician or another person of influence. I expect the name was given for the purpose of trying to intimidate me into forgetting the action I was about to take against them. In retrospect, I guess it's only human nature to defend one's reputation using whatever means are readily available.

I recall one incident when I confronted a man who was endangering his own children by forcing them into a boat that barely floated, without any life preservers on board. This happened on a remote mountain pond, right after ice-out in the early spring.

As I was writing out the well-deserved summons for this nimrod, he launched into a tirade, claiming that his good buddy, Governor Kenneth Curtis, would definitely be contacting me for harassing him. I should enjoy the day, because my job was going to be short-lived at best!

Then there was the time I'd arrested a couple of night-hunters at one o'clock in the morning. They were driving around in a remote field, flashing a huge spotlight out the window with a loaded twelve-gauge shotgun lying alongside of them. The lame excuse they gave for being far out in a back field at that early-morning hour was that they were simply searching for a country store to purchase some pickles for the hunting camp they were staying at. (Like any of our country stores are open at one a.m.!)

As I quickly placed them under arrest, once again the name of Governor Curtis was thrown into my face. One of the parties involved in this fiasco was supposedly a relative of the governor's. (Hell, I was beginning to wonder what kind of friends and relatives our governor had; it seemed as though every offender I managed to confront either knew the man or was somehow related to him!)

One of the most memorable name-dropping incidents I experienced came one fall evening in 1972. Warden Lowell Thomas had requested my assistance in transporting a couple of offenders to the Waldo County Crowbar Hotel. Lowell had arrested the two men for night-hunting along the North Palermo Road in Freedom after they had fired at a deer in front of him. He thought that by separating the men for the long ride to the Belfast lockup, they might make a few incriminating statements that would help strengthen his case.

"I'd like you to transport Donald, if you would," said Lowell. "I'm missing the shells for the rifle they used. I didn't know but maybe you'd get him chatting along the way, and he'd make some incriminating statements. As of now he refuses to talk to me," Lowell added.

With Donald seated next to me, we struck out for Belfast, some twenty-five miles away. I asked Donald if he'd been warned of his legal rights by Warden Thomas. "You know, the right to remain silent, the right to have an attorney present during questioning, et cetera," I said politely.

"Yes, I was. I don't want to talk to anyone," he said.

I thought, *Okay, it's a long way to Belfast. I'll just poke along without making any noise or conversation whatsoever.* I purposely turned the radio off in the cruiser, making for an extremely quiet and rather boring drive. As we cruised along over the rough country road with only the hum of the engine and the thumping of tires making any noise, I could tell the silence was driving my prisoner crazy. He began fidgeting and moving around in the seat, hoping I'd say something, but I wouldn't give in. Finally, he begged, "Can I talk to you?"

"I thought you didn't want to talk to anyone," I said.

He shook his head miserably.

"If you do talk, Donald, I have to warn you that anything you say can and will be used against you in a court of law."

"I know," he said. "But I hate this damn silence! I don't know why that damned warden arrested me in the first place. I didn't shoot," he said anxiously. "I'm not that kind of guy!" he insisted. "I've got a damn good friend of mine who's a game warden, and he'd never do this to me."

My interest piqued, I glanced over his way and inquired, "Oh, really? Which warden do you know so well?"

"You probably know him. He's from around here," Donald said. "His name is John Ford. Do you know him?"

I quickly turned on the dome light in the cruiser to see if this was anyone I should know. I'd never seen him before.

"Yeah, I know John real well," I said with a devious smirk. "What's your last name again?" I politely inquired.

"I'm Donald Johnson," he said boldly, reaching over to shake my hand in a friendly gesture.

"How long have you known John?" I asked calmly, trying to decide once and for all if I should know this person.

"Oh hell, John and I go back a long ways! We used to chum around together in school, long before he ever became a game warden," Donald said.

By now it was quite obvious that Donald was as full of shit as a Christmas turkey. He was trying to drum up a little sympathy because of the mess he suddenly found himself in, and apparently he felt that throwing out the name of a fellow warden might help his cause.

I let him continue rambling on as I smirked from ear to ear, listening to the line of bull he continued flinging my way. I was actually basking in the glory as Donald talked about what a "great fella" this John Ford was—fair and honest. "He'd never do what this Warden Thomas fella is doing to me—never in a million years!" he barked.

Eventually, Don ran out of stories to tell of the many experiences that he and his pal John had shared together. I never said a word as I drove along on the dark country road.

After a rather long pause, Donald finally inquired, "What's your name, by the way? I never did ask."

Switching on the dome light again, I stared into his eyes, anticipating the response as I said cheerfully, "I'm John Ford!"

Suddenly, there was an eerie silence inside the cruiser. Red-faced and highly embarrassed, my great buddy Donald once again decided he didn't want to talk anymore. The remainder of the journey to Belfast was made in complete silence. I got the impression that perhaps Donald didn't like me as much as he once did.

Welcome to My World

It was June of 1973, and Judy and I were eagerly anticipating a visit from my folks. We were newlyweds, and it was a chance to show off our new home, situated in rural Burnham. A few weeks earlier the department had placed the warden's camp up for sale through a bidding process, and Mrs. Ford and I had fortunately won our bid. Things seemed to be coming together quite well for us as we embarked upon living our dreams.

June was a quiet time of year for Fish and Game activity, so the chances of getting called away while visiting with my folks seemed slim. Besides, I knew that if I had to leave for any reason, my folks would certainly understand, seeing that my stepfather, Verne Walker of Sanford, had recently retired from the Warden Service after twenty-three years of dedicated employment. He knew exactly what the job entailed.

Judy had prepared the house from top to bottom in anticipation of her in-laws' visit. Prior to our recent marriage, the only female in the house had been my German shepherd, Princess. She had traveled north with me as I started my new adventure with the Warden Service. Princess was extremely jealous of Judy's sudden arrival onto the scene. She acted as though one female in the house was quite enough, constantly scowling at my new bride with a look of disgust in her eyes. Somehow I was of the impression the feeling was quite mutual.

I'd allowed Princess to sleep on the beds prior to Judy coming aboard. That practice, however, was quickly forbidden once the castle had acquired its new queen. Needless to say, such a restriction increased the tension between my two female companions. Although it seemed that Princess was abiding by the new rule, we suspected she was still making herself right at home on top of the beds whenever we were gone. (The many dog hairs on the bedspreads were a dead giveaway.) Most of the time, however, Princess slept on the floor or underneath the beds.

One morning, Judy arose just prior to the alarm sounding. As she exited our bedroom, she observed Princess slithering down off the spare bed and onto the floor beside it. My canine companion knew exactly what she was doing as she continued to push the envelope with the new queen of the household. But for the time being, they somehow managed to tolerate one another.

As anticipated, my folks arrived early in the morning. We enjoyed a great day together, reminiscing about the past and talking about the future. Verne enthusiastically talked about the warden's job that had been his life for years, and I excitedly related my own personal experiences thus far in my young career. We took a quick tour of my district, and I pointed out those areas where I'd experienced an adventure or two of my own. Before we knew it, the day was over. It was time for everyone to get a good night's rest.

I told my folks that Princess might join them in their room during the night. I knew they wouldn't mind, seeing as they had given her to me in the first place. They both had a fond connection with the dog and wouldn't mind her company in the least. Exchanging the usual nighttime pleasantries, we finally went to bed.

A short time later I heard a loud crash and the *chi-yies* of my dog crying coming from the spare bedroom where my parents were staying. Jumping out of my own bed to investigate what had happened, I heard my folks laughing as they tried to calm the petrified dog. Apparently the wooden slats holding up their bed had given way, causing the bed to collapse. The sudden crash had scared the hell out of the poor dog sleeping beside it, not to mention what it must have done to my folks. Needless to say, the entire fiasco produced a chuckle or two from everyone after we had calmed poor Princess down. My folks certainly remember their first night in our home.

After repairing the bed, we finally managed to get back to sleep.

I was awakened from a sound sleep at 1:30 a.m. by the telephone ringing in my ear. *Who to hell could be calling this late?* I thought as I reached over to pick up the phone.

"Hello!" I said groggily.

"Hi, John, this is the Maine State Police barracks in Augusta. The Waldo County sheriff's office is requesting that you go to Sanborn Pond in the town of Brooks. Apparently they have a possible drowning down there," the dispatcher calmly stated.

"Who would be drowning at this time of the morning?" I numbly replied, as if I really expected an answer. Completely ignoring my stupid comment, the dispatcher inquired, "Should I tell them you'll be en route soon?"

"Yeah, okay," I said. "Tell them I'll be right out."

By now, everyone in the house was once again wide awake, listening as I bitched and complained about having to go out in the middle of the night.

I quickly headed over to the little pond in Brooks, where I met up with Sheriff Stan Knox and Chief Deputy Roy Thomas. Warden Chandler showed up with his department boat in tow at about the same time. I parked among the tall pines of the parking lot, with the volume of my mobile radio turned up as high as it would go just in case the barracks needed to contact me.

It was a cool night, or should I say early morning. There was a heavy layer of fog floating over the water of the little pond. The sheriff said a group of inebriated revelers had gone to the pond for a late-night swim. After cooling themselves off, they went to Belfast, where they noticed one of the group was missing. Kenneth was last seen swimming in front of the dam in about eight feet of water. After agreeing that no one ever saw him exit the water, they believed he may have drowned.

Warden Chandler and I unloaded his boat at the nearby landing, readying it for the search. I had an eerie feeling as the wind blew the fog off from the water and onto us. There was that hard-to-describe smell of death in the air that always seemed to be present at one of these incidents.

With a bright handheld light, I draped myself out over the bow of Warden Chandler's boat as we started searching the shallow waters near the dam where the victim was last seen. I could plainly see the rocky bottom of the pond as we slowly circled the area. Suddenly, in about six feet of water, I spotted the legs of a man clad in his underwear, lying facedown below us.

"There he is," I said to Chandler. He shut off the motor and tried to hold us in one spot. Using a long pole with a small metal hook attached to it, we went about recovering the victim. Together we were able to snag the back of his shorts, slowly hoisting him back up to the surface. I was able to grab onto the body and float it back in to shore.

Once the body was recovered, the local medical examiner was notified to come to the scene. He would have to legally pronounce the man dead and rule whether or not the cause of death warranted an investigation. We all stood near the corpse, shooting the breeze and waiting for the medical examiner to arrive. By the time all of the legalities were finally taken care of, it was nearly 3:30 in the morning.

Suddenly, everyone had left the area, leaving me the last one in the parking lot. I slowly walked back to my cruiser beneath the large pine trees. The fog was thick, and I could hear the breeze blowing through the pine branches overhead. There was an air of uneasiness in the strange and eerie silence, and I picked up the pace a bit, anxious to reach the serenity of my cruiser.

I was thinking about the bizarre circumstances surrounding this incident, wondering if every-thing was aboveboard in this fiasco. Was this death truly accidental, or something else? There seemed to be a calmness and a serious lack of concern from the victim's friends that I was finding a bit bothersome. Ultimately, it wasn't my case to worry about, as the sheriff's department was in charge of the investigation. Despite my suspicions, there were never any charges filed.

Finally, I was safely inside my cruiser, ready to fire up the engine and depart the isolated area. I'd forgotten all about the volume of my mobile radio being on high, in case the barracks needed to contact me. At about that time, the dispatcher decided to check on my status. His loud voice scared the living hell out of me. Foolishly, I let out a blat that would have shaken the bravest of souls had they been standing there.

It was close to four a.m. when I finally returned home. Once again, everyone woke up as I dragged myself back into the house. It was rather obvious that we all were lacking a good night's rest.

My folks didn't hang around very long before deciding to venture back down the pike from whence they'd come. They'd gotten another taste of what the old days had been like for them, and they obviously wanted no part of it. They'd already paid their dues!

Come to think of it, after their brief visit, they never did come back to our little camp out in the middle of nowhere. I wonder why?

Smell the Hands

It was 8:30 p.m. on a June night when a Unity Plantation citizen complained about shots being fired below his house. "I just had a car go down past my residence, John. It had two shady-acting duffers in it. I know one of these individuals to be a poacher from way back. I think they've just shot a deer down in my back field, and I bet they're down there gutting it right now," he said.

It happened to be my day off, but when it came to catching poachers, there was no such thing. It seemed a bit early in the year for anyone to be poaching deer, but then again, a few weeks prior to this complaint I had arrested my buddy Arthur and his cronies for jacking, so this could be the real deal.

Gary Parsons, who was pursuing his dream of becoming a game warden himself, happened to be visiting when the call came in.

"Want to go catch some poachers, Gary?" I asked. (To even ask such a question was about as stupid as asking a patron at a house of ill repute if he was waiting there for sex.) Hell, if I'd refused to respond to this complaint, Gary would've made me feel guilty. "Are you neglecting your duties?" I could hear him saying. It was this type of enthusiastic dedication from young men like Gary Parsons and Jim Ross, another aspiring young warden, that often spurred me on to work more hours than expected. In those days, people who were interested in becoming a game warden, or who just wanted to come along for a possible adventure, were allowed to ride along with us game wardens.

Of course, the moments of excited anticipation before going out in the field and the enjoyment of holding bad guys responsible for their sins did help in maintaining my level of enthusiasm. Gary and Jim both had the same burning desire to become game wardens that I myself once had, and I wanted to see them achieve their goals. (In fact, years later, Jim actually became my boss.)

In 1974, I was exceptionally busy responding to poaching complaints. It was obvious that the rules and regulations designed to protect and preserve our deer herd were somewhat ineffective. After all, I'd just corralled a bunch of night-hunters in May, and here I was, a few weeks later, responding to yet another complaint. It was highly unusual, since this type of complaint was typically unheard of until early August. This year's activities seemed to be starting much earlier.

Perhaps I should have been talking to my legislative buddy, Ken "Babe" Tozier, from Troy, advising him that the penalties for poaching were way too lenient, and no longer seemed much of a deterrent for those who insisted on breaking the rules. . . . Nah, I didn't want to do that; I was having way too much fun trying to catch these guys.

Gary and I quickly headed off to Unity Plantation, hoping to make yet another bust. When we arrived in the complainant's dooryard, he stated that the vehicle hadn't returned as of yet. He was quite sure they'd shot a deer.

"Probably it was that little spike-horn buck in velvet that I've seen coming out there every night about this time," he griped bitterly.

Dusk was settling in as Gary and I headed on foot into the area where these men were supposedly located. I quickly found a car tucked away on a woods road adjacent to a large field. We decided to watch the vehicle and wait for them to return, so we hunkered down in the brush alongside of it. The mosquitoes were unbearable as they swarmed around us, sucking our blood by the pint. We didn't dare swat at them, fearing any movement might alert the poachers of our presence. I was willing to sacrifice a little blood and a whole lot of itching for the chance to capture these devilish critters.

It was near dark when two men finally walked out of the woods at the far end of the field. As they slowly walked our way, I could see that one of them was toting a rifle while the other one appeared to be dragging something behind him.

Adrenaline began flowing through my veins as I anticipated what the next few minutes might bring. It's hard to describe what it feels like when you're dealing with armed violators.

As these men slowly headed our way, the fellow dragging what I assumed to be a deer carcass detoured over to the edge of the roadway. He hid whatever he was dragging in the tall grass adjacent to the highway, marking the spot by placing a beer bottle upright on the edge of the pavement. Completing the task, he rejoined his buddy and they returned to their vehicle. As they walked toward their car, I was able to identify them as Richard and Alan, two well-known poachers in the area.

It was time to announce my presence.

"Game warden, fellas—hold it right there!" I yelled as I stepped out of the brush. "I'll take that for the time being," I said, quickly taking possession of the loaded, high-powered rifle Alan was toting.

"Doing a little hunting, are we?" I asked.

Nervously, Richard replied, "Yup. We shot at a woodchuck a while ago. Apparently we missed him, though, 'cause we c-c-couldn't find him," he stuttered.

It was so obvious he was lying. His hands trembled uncontrollably and he was unable to look me in the face when he spoke.

"Oh, really?" I said. "Your woodchuck wouldn't

happen to have had a set of antlers, now, would it?" I chuckled.

"Oh no, sir, that would be illegal, and we w-w-wouldn't do anything like that," Richard said humbly. "Here, look at my hands," he offered. "There's no blood, no hair—no evidence of a deer. Check it out!"

He was right. I examined both of the men's hands, and there was absolutely no sign of deer hair or blood connecting them to any crime.

"Well, boys, either you've washed up extremely well, or maybe I'm terribly mistaken, but I think we ought to take a little hike out to the edge of the road and see what kind of a woodchuck you dragged out of there. Whaddya say?" I said.

They never said a word as we slowly walked over to the roadway.

"What have we here?" I asked, as I lit up the carcass of a small spike-horn buck, hidden in the tall grass.

"I guess you've got us," Richard conceded.

"I'm placing you both under arrest for hunting deer in closed season," I calmly informed them.

They were extremely cooperative and very friendly.

"I was hoping you'd send us on our way when you couldn't find anything on our hands," Richard said, snickering. "You're pretty observant for a rookie warden, but I'm going to let you in on a little secret you might want to remember for future reference: A good poacher is careful not to leave any telltale signs of the crime on his body—you know, things like deer hair and blood. I carefully washed off any evidence, just in case we happened to get stopped by someone like you on the way out of here," he bragged. "I didn't know you were watching me drag the damn thing up to the roadway to be picked up later on. I probably should have left it back in the woods, but even I get careless sometimes.

"Now, here's my advice to you," Richard continued. "Whenever you suspect someone has just killed and gutted a deer, ask to smell their hands. You can wash away all the blood and the hair in the world, but that damned old deer-paunch smell will stay with you for a while," he said, chuckling some more.

With that, he shoved his hands underneath my nose to prove his point. "Smell my hands! See, I told you so. That paunch smell just can't be washed away," he said, laughing as my nose wrinkled from the putrid smell.

He was absolutely right; the smell was obvious. Tonight this baby game warden learned a valuable lesson from an old poacher. I could see it all now: "You have the right to remain silent. You have the right to blah, blah, blah. Now, let me smell your hands!"

I sent Gary after my cruiser as I monitored my prisoners and gathered up the evidence. Together we stuffed the dead deer in the trunk and the two poachers in the backseat of the cruiser, and headed for the local lockup in Waterville.

Both Richard and Alan appeared before the judge the very next morning, paying $200 each for their sins. Justice had been meted out and quickly served.

From that moment on, I decided that if a suspect gave me a one-fingered salute, I just might have to ask him if I could smell it.

For Better or Worse

I received a phone call from a rather distraught lady from Troy one early evening in August. "Are you the game warden?" she inquired.

"Yes, ma'am. What can I help you with?" I responded.

"Well, if someone is shooting deer out of season and bringing them home, are you the one I call to have them arrested?" she asked.

My interest was piqued. "Yes, ma'am, I'm the one who would investigate the crime. Do you know someone who is doing such a thing?" I inquired, wondering where this conversation was headed.

"I certainly do, and gawd-dammit, I'm sick and tired of it!" she shouted over the phone.

By now, I was listening intently, hoping this call might have some merit. "Well, if you'll fill me in on who you think is doing this, I'd be more than happy to investigate," I said. I figured the person calling was probably some irate neighbor living next door to a poacher, or possibly someone with a score to settle against a rival.

"You're damn right I'll tell you," she said. "He's probably gonna kill me, but I'm sick and tired of it. He and his buddy drink all night long and go night-hunting, and then they bring their damn deer back here to cut up whenever they feel like it," she said.

"I don't blame you for being upset," I said, hoping to entice her into telling me a little more. "Just who is this culprit that has you so cranked up?" I inquired.

"It's Bubba, that gawd-damned husband of mine, and his drinking buddy, Liston. They're drunk most of the time. Whenever they go off on one of their drinking binges they always drag a deer back home, messing up my house. Then I'm petrified that you're going to step through the door, hauling us all off to jail. I'm some damned sick and tired of it," she said.

This was a touchy situation, I realized—one that could have severe repercussions if not handled correctly. I sure as hell wouldn't want to be held responsible for a wife-beating, a divorce, or possibly even murder, all because of a dead deer or two. I could see the front-page headline now: HUSBAND KILLS WIFE OVER DEAD DEER. I'd never be able to live with myself should that happen.

"How often is this happening, ma'am? When's the last time they brought a deer home?"

"Would you believe almost weekly? The last time they dragged one home is right now," she screamed. "Damn it all, that husband of mine is presently passed out on the couch, and his buddy Liston passed out in our bedroom. I've had it!" she said. "I don't care what he does, I simply can't keep living like this. You have to do something to help me out here."

"Well, for starters, I need to know where you're located, and whether or not you'll give me written permission to search your home for a dead deer," I said.

"Damn it, I wouldn't have called you if I wasn't willing to give you all the information you need," she shouted.

With that, she told me exactly where she lived. She said her husband had shot a small doe the previous night, the second one in a week. Most of the critter was cut up, but her kitchen floor was covered with deer blood, and the hindquarters, heart, and liver were all stuffed into her refrigerator. The front quarters of the animal were in a nearby freezer.

"The rifle used to kill the deer is still loaded and leaning up against the wall in the shed," she said. "I've got a good mind to use the damn thing on him if he doesn't smarten to hell up. I'd like to kick his arse out of here, but I know I won't. You come up here and I'll sign any papers you need. I just want him to be taught a lesson."

"Well, I'm perfectly willing to do so, ma'am, but how do you think he's going to react, when and if he finds out it was you who turned him in?" I inquired.

"Oh, he'll be madder than hell at first, but he'll get over it," she said.

"Do you think he'll get violent, or possibly turn against you?" I asked.

"I don't care if he does," she said. "I've had enough. I'm going to move out for a few days, once you cart him off to jail. It'll give him a little time to cool off. One way or the other, he'll either smarten up or I'll just leave. I can't stand it anymore."

She was obviously expecting me to solve her immediate problem, and as I headed for Troy, I realized it was a task I was willing to assume. Arriving at the residence, I was greeted at the door by a very determined lady who quickly signed a consent form authorizing me to search her home for evidence of a crime, including deer parts or any other evidence.

"You don't have to worry about them bothering you," she stated. "They're both still passed out. I doubt if you could wake them up with a stick of dynamite."

I assured her I'd do everything I could to protect her identity, but more than likely he'd eventually surmise that she'd been the one to turn them in.

"I know he will—and I don't intend to hide it from him one bit. He can either straighten up, or one of us is shipping out," she said firmly. "The time has come for him to start acting like the husband I married, or else he can find a new life.

I'm not putting up with it any longer. If this is what it takes to shock him into reality, so be it. If not, he can start all over again with someone else who's willing to put up with his bullshit!"

Escorting me into the run-down home, she quickly took me to the refrigerator, exposing the deer parts I was looking for. It was obvious the deer had been dragged into the kitchen for butchering, as evidenced by the dried blood trail spread across the floor.

She then led me into the living room where her husband was passed out on the couch, completely oblivious to the fact that his world was about to change. Slumped across the bed in the next room was Liston, her husband's buddy. He, too, was in his own little dreamland, totally unaware of what was happening around him. Next, she took me out to the shed to see the rifle she'd mentioned.

"There, damn it! Have you seen enough?" she asked when we'd returned to the dooryard.

I responded, "Yup, I reckon I have."

I then persuaded her to grab some clothing and leave the residence so she'd be out of harm's way as I went about performing my duties of seizing the deer and arresting the responsible culprits.

"You mean, I can't stand here and watch you drag him to hell out of there wearing them tight handcuffs around his scrawny wrists?" she inquired.

Chuckling at her request, I said, "I'd rather you weren't here; it would make it easier for both of us."

"Okay," she reluctantly conceded. She grabbed an already-packed suitcase and headed out the door.

I quickly went about my business of gathering up the deer parts and securing the loaded rifle from the shed. It was show-and-tell time for hubby and Liston, so I began shaking them, desperately trying to awaken them from their deep sleep.

One by one, I managed to bring them back to reality. It was quite obvious they'd had a lot to drink. Fortunately, they were good-natured drunks and not the fighting kind. They were the type who would simply grin and bear it if the world was collapsing around them.

I attempted to read them their rights, but they were too busy sputtering and mumbling to each other to understand any of my legal ramblings. Bubba's first words, once he'd rubbed his eyes and regained some semblance of awareness, were, "Uh-oh . . . you're that gawd-damned game warden, aren't you? That damned old bitch—she really did turn us in, didn't she?"

He knew exactly what had happened. Apparently it was something she'd threatened to do for quite some time.

"Oh well, I knew it was only a matter of time," he said. "I love that woman, you know. I really do!

So Mr. Warden, how much is this gonna cost me?"

"I don't know as though I'd worry so much about the money as I would about your marriage, Bubba," I said. "If you love her as much as you say, that may be the biggest problem you're facing right now. She's ready to leave you, you know?"

"Nah, that's no problem," he said. "Hell, she turned me in for drunk driving not too long ago. I'm just now getting my license back and getting the fine paid off from that damn fiasco. We'll work it out. She'll be home in a few days, proud as a peacock for what she's done," he chuckled. "Feisty little devil, ain't she?"

I picked up Bubba and Liston from the county jail the next morning, taking them both before Judge Smith, where they each pleaded guilty to illegal possession of deer. The judge ordered them to pay a fine of $200 each for their sins, granting them plenty of time to raise the money.

Afterward, I escorted them back to Troy, where all of their problems had started a mere twenty-four hours earlier.

A few days later I drove by the residence, noting that Bubba's wife had returned. Judging from the friendly wave I received from the couple, it appeared as if things were on the mend. This was country living as it existed in the foothills of Troy, Maine.

You had to love it. I know I did!

Two Times a Loser

Arthur, one of my old poaching buddies who liked to tantalize me every chance he got, was yet another example of what goes around, comes around.

When I'd first arrived in the area, Arthur had taken advantage of my youth at the Bither Brook smelt run when he and the rest of his crew had casually enticed me into drinking a hefty amount of Arthur's favorite home brew. They wanted to test my social standing and see whether I dared to befriend them or not.

Damn, it was good brew, but sadly, I don't recall a thing that happened that night. I awoke the next morning, lying on my couch with my pants half on and half off. For all I knew, the smelters could have walked away with every damned smelt in the brook on that cold spring night, and I wouldn't have cared. I'd been set up by Arthur and his cronies, but I knew there would be a day of reckoning. It was just a matter of time. Besides, I really couldn't blame them for my own stupidity and vulnerability, and for wanting to be accepted. I wanted to make a bunch of new friends on that night, and I did just that!

Arthur constantly bragged of his poaching activities to anyone who would listen, myself included. I remember joking with him on many occasions, "Arthur, it's a long road with no turns in it, old boy, and when you mess up, I plan on being there!"

Well, Arthur messed up in 1974—not once, but twice. The first time was Memorial Day weekend in 1974. Gary Parsons and I were working night-hunters in Unity after an informant had complained the night before about someone illuminating the fields and firing at deer. Deciding that perhaps they'd return again the following evening, we decided to watch the area. It seemed awfully early for anyone to be involved in night-hunting, but I'd learned in this business that you just never know.

Shortly after our arrival a car slowly cruised by us, flashing a bright spotlight from one side of the road to the other, obviously looking for a whitetail. When I stopped the vehicle I found my buddy Arthur, his girlfriend, and his closest buddy, Frankie, perched inside. Neatly tucked between Arthur's legs was a rifle and the spotlight they'd been using to illuminate the fields. I immediately arrested the trio for night-hunting, but was unable to find the shells for the rifle. Arthur wisely claimed to have left the ammo at home, a story about as believable as if he'd said the moon was made out of Swiss cheese.

Arthur and his pals claimed to be returning from an evening of fishing in Freedom. This part of his story was believable, seeing as there were fishing poles and fresh bait in the car, plus Arthur was wearing those old rubber chest-waders that he often wore when fishing—the same waders I'd seen so many times before as he stood around the bonfire at the Bither Brook smelt run.

"You don't need a rifle to fish, do you, Arthur?" I asked.

"Nope, not really, John, but I believe it is legal to have one in the car, isn't it?" he responded.

"It doesn't help your cause, to be lighting the fields and holding the rifle in your lap," I said, smiling.

"Now don't tell me that's illegal too, especially without ammo!" he barked.

Arthur wanted to go to the bathroom in the worst way, but I refused to let him. I surmised that if given the chance he would toss any ammo he might have out into the black of night.

Eventually at the county jail, Arthur was ordered to take off his chest-waders, which he was hesitant to do. "What if I refuse?" he said.

I informed him they'd come off, one way or another, either with his help or without; the choice was his.

"Why, Arthur, there wouldn't be something hidden inside that you wouldn't want me to see, by any chance?" I inquired.

"Of course not," he grumbled as he slowly

pulled the boots off, one after the other. *Ka-plunk,* out onto the floor dropped a rifle clip with five live rounds of ammo. It was the final piece of evidence I needed to cinch the charge of night-hunting.

"Oh, for Christ's sake, John, you knew they were there all the time," he said with a sheepish grin.

"Uh-huh, I kinda did, Arthur, I kinda did . . . and I figure that old road without a turn in it has come my way tonight, don't you, bud?" I asked proudly.

"Reckon you're right, John Boy—I reckon you're right."

Arthur's luck took another turn for the worse in November of that year, when he, his brother, and two of their cronies were bagged for night-hunting in Knox. It was the second time around for Arthur that year.

I reminded him of my earlier statement: "When you mess up, Arthur, hopefully I'll be there!" Yup, there was a whole lot of truth to the old saying of what goes around, comes around. I liked playing the game of cat and mouse, and was more than happy to occasionally be the winner.

Pretty Damn Sharp, Wasn't He, John?

Previously I introduced you to the so-called modern-day Robin Hood named Grover, perhaps the most talked-about and notorious poacher roaming the central Maine area. After many conversations with the local citizenry, listening to their complaints about Grover and his gang of warriors, I knew it would only be a matter of time before I'd be confronting them on official business. That occasion occurred during the early-morning hours of an October day in 1970.

Warden Norman Gilbert and I were parked along the Albion Road in Unity, patiently waiting for night-hunting activity to venture our way. Norman had heard the same tales and fears about Grover and his gang that I had, but he hadn't met him yet either.

Even though I'd told Norman about the fairly cordial conversation I'd had with Grover a few days earlier at the local garage, Norman made it perfectly clear that he didn't trust the poacher, or his cohorts. "Should we be forced to deal with any of them in an official capacity, it's not going to end well! I've heard too damn much stuff about these guys, and none of it was good," he said. Norman was thoroughly convinced that

Grover was every bit the treacherous and intimidating individual everyone described, and needed to be handled with extreme caution. There was no convincing my partner that his fears were completely unfounded and highly exaggerated.

"I think his bark is far worse than his bite," I said to Norman, but my words fell on deaf ears.

"I'm telling you, John, I don't trust him! You've heard what these people are saying. It's not all made up, you know! Just look at his background."

On that particular night, we sat in the cruiser, observing the fields along a rural stretch of highway. Suddenly, a vehicle came our way at a fairly fast clip, casting a bright beam of light directly into the fields surrounding us. During this time of the year, state law forbade attempting to illuminate wild game from one half-hour after sunset to one half-hour before sunrise. Seeing as where it was nearly 1:30 a.m., this was a definite violation of that law. Considering the hour, there was also a good possibility these folks might have a rifle and ammo with them, and they just might be night-hunting.

I immediately pulled out behind the vehicle as it passed by, driving without my headlights. This stealth mode was necessary in order for us to sneak up behind them without their suspecting anyone being around. Such a mode of operation creates an element of surprise and often prevents a high-speed chase; plus, it allows us to see if any evidence is tossed out the window.

Sneaking in behind them rather quickly, I initiated my headlights, the flashing blue emergency lights, and the blaring siren, signaling for them to stop. The peace and tranquility of the quiet Unity night air was shattered. Instead of stopping as required by law, they increased their speed for a short distance. Norman began yelling, "They're throwing stuff out the window!" I immediately recognized the battered old blue GMC truck belonging to Grover. It was the same old dented wreck I'd seen at the local garage just a few days earlier. There were three occupants thrashing around in the cab of the truck as they slowly pulled over to the side of the road before coming to a stop. I told Norman, "That's Grover and his crew!" as we both bailed out of the cruiser, heading their way.

As I sauntered up to the driver's side of the truck, Grover gruffly demanded, "What the hell are you stopping us for?"

I barked back, "For starters, Grover, we're going to be citing all three of you for illuminating those fields back there."

"Illuminating fields!" he yelled. "Are you #$@%*& nuts! Do you see any gawd-damned light in here?" he yelled defiantly. "This is nothing more than #$@%*& harassment, and you know it! You'll never be able to prove it in a court of law, and I intend to fight it all the way if I have to."

Norman directed me to get identification from all three of them and to issue them summonses for the illuminating violation. He quickly scurried back to the cruiser, calling for additional assistance; he was thoroughly convinced we were going to be in a bad mess before all was said and done.

I secured Grover and the second man's identification as they continued sputtering and grousing about being stopped. When I asked for identification from the third individual, he rather politely stated, "I don't have any identification on me, sir. I left it at home." He was by far the politest and most cooperative of the three. Up to this point, he also seemed to be the most sensible. I gladly returned the same respect he was giving me as I asked him his name, address, and date of birth, in order to complete the court summons I was issuing.

"Yes, sir; my name is Leonard."

"Leonard what?" I asked, as I quickly jotted down the information on a piece of paper.

"Leonard Sharpe," he politely responded.

I inquired, "How do you spell your last name, Leonard?"

"S-H-A-R-P-E," he said slowly. By now, he was starting to get a little more arrogant and defensive. "Did you get that okay?" he asked.

"I got it, Leonard," I shot back. "You don't have to get irritated with me; I'm only trying to save you fellows a trip to jail, so I'd strongly suggest that you cool it a bit, or you may find yourself headed for the county lockup after all!"

Grover chuckled in his usual self-satisfied way. "Jail, jail—for lighting a field without a light! Now that'll be a tough case to prove in court, won't it?"

"Grover, I assure you, we'll find that light you threw out the window, and perhaps a little more, such as possibly a rifle and ammunition," I said. "Just so you are aware of it, should we find a firearm, these charges will be upgraded to the more-serious offense of night-hunting. You do understand that, don't you?"

By now, several more wardens and a couple of state troopers had arrived at the scene. The road was lined with flashing blue lights. Norman, seeing my reaction, said he'd thought it best to have some help standing by just in case we needed it. I was a bit embarrassed about having such a large entourage lining the roadway, giving the appearance that a major catastrophe had just occurred. But if it made Norman feel a bit more at ease, all the better. I also reckoned we could use a little extra help in retracing the route of travel, searching for the light and possibly a firearm that could've been thrown out the window of the speeding truck.

I quickly completed the three summonses for Grover, Billy, and Leonard, charging them with illegally illuminating fields before sending them on their way.

Grover smirked as I passed the court papers in through the window. "I'm telling you, boys, you're wasting your time searching for a light, a gun, or anything else. We didn't have any of those things, and we sure as hell didn't do anything wrong! Harassment, that's all it is." He continued yelling as he quickly shifted the truck into gear and sped away from the area.

With plenty of assistance now available, we conducted a methodical search, retracing the route traveled by Grover and his crew. In no time, Norman had found a large handheld spotlight lying on top of the frost-covered ground, the type that plugged into a vehicle's cigarette lighter. We found it in the grass a short distance from where we'd first observed them, and with this item, we had retrieved the physical evidence needed for clinching the illuminating charge in court, as we continued searching for a firearm and ammunition.

We never found anything else along the route, not to say that it wasn't there. The distance they'd traveled had afforded them plenty of places to toss out a firearm and shells, but it was like looking for a needle in a haystack.

In November, both Grover and Billy arrived at

the district court for their court appearances, where they pleaded not guilty, requesting a trial before the judge. Leonard failed to appear in court that morning, ignoring the summons that had been given to him. Consequently, an arrest warrant was quickly issued by the judge for Leonard Sharpe. Billy and Grover were convicted later that day after a brief trial. The judge listened to all of the testimony and quickly ruled against them with a guilty decision. A fine of $35 each was assessed to both men. Had the night-hunting charge been included, the penalty for such an offense at that time was a mere $200.

As we exited the courtroom, Grover came my way with a silly smirk on his face and said, "No hard feelings, John! I told you I'd fight you tooth and nail in court, and I did. You won this one!" Then, with his customary loud chuckle, Grover shouted so that everyone around could hear him, "Now just where do you suppose old Lenny is, John?"

"I don't have a clue where he is, Grover. Do you?"

Winking at me as he slowly walked away, sporting a big smile on his face, he loudly said, "Well, I don't know where to hell he is right now John, but he sure as hell was some gawd-damned *sharp,* wasn't he? Ha ha ha!" He continued chuckling to himself all the way down the hallway and out through the door, as he muttered over and over, "Yup, old Lenny was some damn sharp! Ha ha ha!"

I realized I'd been had. Leonard's last name—maybe even his first name—was nothing more than an alias used for his convenience during the stop. This rookie warden had accepted his answer as honest when he'd claimed he had no identification with him. Grover was right: Lenny was some damned sharp! He had skated scot-free from the charges, while Grover and Billy were held accountable for their sins. To this very day, tucked away somewhere in the files, is an arrest warrant for Leonard Sharpe, wherever, and whoever, he might be.

While I may have won my first official confrontation against Grover, it was he and his buddies who had managed to pull the wool over my eyes in the end. I couldn't help but laugh along with them, for obviously I wasn't quite as sharp as they were. Through it all, I sensed that Grover and I had developed a little rapport after all—an understanding that contained a little mutual respect along with a subtle sort of friendship.

Our paths would officially cross many more times in the future, sometimes quite contentiously, and other times, rather cordially. Grover seemed to realize I never took any of his actions personally, and likewise, he made it clear he would fight me all the way in court if I ever caught any of them doing something wrong.

Grover unwittingly confirmed my feeling that we were developing some mutual respect one day, shortly after the hunting season had officially ended and during one of our little roadside chats. He said, "There's no reason I can't like you ten months out of the year, John. It's just during the months of October and November when I'd rather not see you around!"

The Lead-Pipe Hat Attack

One October evening, wannabe warden Gary Parsons and I were working night-hunters in the town of Montville, always noted for its fair share of sheer excitement. This night would prove to be no exception. We were tucked away in a little hideout, monitoring a series of fields located along the so-called Center Road. It was an extremely dark and moonless night as we patiently waited for action to come our way. This area was highly noted for its abundance of deer, and more so, its illegal night-hunting activity.

Approximately two years earlier, while working this same location with Warden Langdon "Smalley" Chandler, the night had ended in an exhilarating chase that resulted in a collision with the culprits. The excitement of that night almost cost me my right to ever broadcast over the State Police radio ever again.

Gary was all but asleep on this night when I happened to notice a vehicle a short distance away on another road, driving around in a remote field. They were illuminating the area with a huge spotlight.

"Night-hunters, night-hunters!" I shouted, nearly causing the slumbering Gary to launch himself through the roof of my cruiser.

"Where?" he groggily inquired. I pointed to where the illegal activity was occurring.

"I know exactly where they're at!" I said as we shot down the road like a rocket heading for its target. "I hope we can get there before they leave."

Turning onto a narrow dirt road, I was driving without headlights so as not to alert the offenders of my pending approach. "Aha, we're in time," I said. They were still driving around in the back of the field, flashing a bright light out the side window, obviously searching for the yellow eyes of a deer. I blocked the only exit out of the field, anxiously awaiting their arrival back at our location. My heart was pounding like a drunken drummer beating on a large steel drum as I once again anticipated what kind of excitement the next few minutes might bring.

Eventually, the vehicle crested a small knoll directly in front of us. Upon observing my cruiser blocking their escape route, they skidded to an abrupt halt a short distance away. There were three adult men in the pickup truck, obviously pondering what action to take next.

Quickly exiting the cruiser, I ran toward them, intending to make an arrest. Suddenly, they stomped on the gas and headed straight for me. I retreated like a scared rabbit fleeing from a hungry fox. I certainly was no match for the tons of steel rapidly bearing down upon me. Just as I opened the door of my cruiser, seeking shelter, they struck it a glancing blow. The brute force of the collision tossed my body hard up against the side of the car. I thought I'd broken both of my legs as I watched them sail on by.

They bounced up over the rock wall behind us and out onto the narrow dirt road where they raced away, lickety-split. Limping inside the cruiser, I spun around in the damp grass, speeding after them in hot pursuit. I quickly notified the dispatchers of my situation, requesting that any available assistance be sent my way.

"Those sons of bitches tried to run me over, Gary! If that isn't the use of deadly force, then by jeez, I don't know what the hell is!" I screamed as we raced down the narrow dirt road at break-neck speed. By then, Gary was sucked down into the seat of my cruiser like a toilet plunger solidly hooked onto a wet ceramic bowl. His fingers were firmly dug into the dashboard and I noticed he wasn't uttering a word.

I followed the thick cloud of dust in front of us, quickly catching up to the offender's tail-lights. We slid out onto the Thompson Ridge Road at racetrack speeds. I was directly behind them as we shot down the dusty road like a couple of bullets chasing each other.

Thankfully, I was familiar with the area known as the Plantation, and I knew the layout of the road ahead. We were approaching a section of highway where the road made a 90-degree turn. We slid around the sharp curve nearly sideways as I caught up to their back bumper.

I told Gary, "I've had enough of this bullshit!" The adrenaline was flowing into my veins by the quart as I pulled up alongside the fleeing truck. Almost exactly like the chase of a few years earlier, we kind of collided with each other. Skidding around in the middle of the road we came to a rather sudden and very abrupt stop.

The blaring siren shattered the serenity of the area, and a cloud of dust quickly filled the air. The door flew open on the passenger's side of the truck and one of the passengers bailed out of the vehicle and ran into a nearby field. I quickly arrested the operator, a fellow named Walt.

As I was securing him in the backseat of my cruiser, Gary yelled, "John, you've got a guy hightailing it up the road with a rifle in his hands!" Instructing Gary to keep an eye on Walt, I quickly caught up to a man named Lee as he desperately tried to flee the scene. It was almost a comical sight to watch (notice that I said *almost*).

Lee was quite inebriated, and he had to struggle to make his little legs carry him along. For every step he took forward, he went backwards two more. After a brief and rather uneventful confrontation, I was able to gain control of both Lee and the loaded rifle, and I quickly confined him in the backseat of my cruiser alongside his buddy Walt.

One more to go!

As Gary stood by the cruiser guarding my captives, I headed out across the field, searching for the final escapee. I spotted him lurking nearby. Like his other buddies, he was also highly intoxicated, but his mood was much more violent than theirs. Screeching at the top of his lungs, he yelled, "C'mon out here, you son of a bitch! I'll make you a friggin' hat with this #$@%*& lead pipe!" All the while he was screaming he was swinging a large lead pipe around his head in a very threatening manner.

"C'mon, you gawd-damned #$@%*&!" he shouted. "Come out here so I can make this pipe a permanent fixture of your big fat #$@%*& head!" He certainly wasn't being any too sociable, that was for sure! I thought to myself, *This is a hell of a way to greet someone who is simply trying to do his job.*

Now I have to say, my momma didn't raise a complete idiot, although some might consider that debatable. I figured I had two of the three culprits in custody and perhaps it was time to await the arrival of a little more assistance before making the final roundup—assistance that was hopefully headed my way. I wasn't about to personally confront this pipe-swinging drunk who wanted to make me a new customized hat.

If I got much closer than I already was, it would soon become a hat attack, so I wisely maintained a cautious buffer zone, watching the performance from a safe place.

Off in the distance I heard the wailing sirens as the calvalry came streaming into the area. Heading up the charge was none other than my trooper buddy, Harry Bailey, followed by Sheriff Stan Knox and his chief deputy, Leroy Thomas, from the Waldo County sheriff's office. They were followed by a small flotilla of officers, all rallying to the aid of one of their own. God, what a handsome and welcome sight they were. I could have kissed them all!

The next few minutes consisted of a somewhat vocal standoff with Terry, the pipe-swinging hoodlum, which had moved down into his dooryard, located nearby. In due time, Terry was persuaded into dropping the pipe and peacefully accompanying his buddies to the local lockup. It was smooth-talking Harry Bailey who convinced him to do that. (Everyone always listened to Harry!)

Terry, Walt, and Lee had provided yet another exciting night in Montville for the local game warden. Other than a few bumps and bruises from being tossed up against the side of the cruiser like a Ping-Pong ball, I was none the worse for wear, and I had a few more memories to record in my diary.

"Which One of You Damn Kids . . ."

My cruising buddy Jim Ross, who at this time was still just a guy interested in the profession, was my traveling companion one lovely day in May. We were checking fishermen on the causeway at Sandy Pond in Freedom, a small stretch of roadway heading onto an island located at the western end of Sandy Pond. This remote fishing spot was well known for its illegal activities, including folks fishing over the limit, having no fishing licenses, or a variety of other wildlife infractions. Because of its secluded location, most people felt quite safe in this area.

The fishing rules prohibited the possession of bass during this time of year, as they were extremely vulnerable to capture while lying upon their gravel spawning beds, scattered along lake shorelines. It was easy to capture one of these fish simply by casting a lure into the middle of their nest. In order to protect the eggs, the adult fish would quickly grab onto anything invading its territory, carrying it away from the area. If this type of fishing activity were allowed, it easily might deplete the bass population. The well-publicized rules made it illegal to possess any bass until after June 20, when the spawning season was basically completed and the fish moved into deeper waters.

As we cruised into the area, we noticed a van parked on the causeway with a man fishing all by himself at the far end of the graveled structure. Running along the shoreline were half a dozen young kids who obviously had lost interest in fishing. Either that, or they'd never had any interest to begin with.

"We'll hide the cruiser, grab the binoculars, and watch him from off in the distance for a while," I said to Jim. "You never know what we might see."

This fisherman didn't have a clue we were watching his every move. He was casting his lure into one specific area a short distance away from where he was standing. It wasn't the normal cast-and-retrieve action—more like he was trying to place his lure into the same exact spot with every cast. Suddenly he set the hook and the water exploded with a large bass, desperately trying to shake the pointed lure from its mouth.

Jimmy said, "Wow, he's got a bass, and it's a nice one!"

"It sure is!" I muttered. "It's rather obvious that he's located a bass bed in front of him by the way he's trying to drop that lure into the same spot on every cast."

Quickly reeling the fish into shore, he removed the hook from its jaw, cautiously looking around to see if anyone was watching him. Even his own kids weren't paying any attention as he scurried over to the backside of the van, holding the fish firmly in his hands. Scanning the area once again to see if anyone might be watching, he quickly opened the rear door of the van, climbed inside, hoisted up the spare tire, and gently placed the bass underneath it. Judging from his actions, he obviously knew he was violating the law.

Clambering back out of the van, he returned to his fishing pole and started searching the shoreline for yet another bass bed.

"This ought to be interesting!" I said to Jim. "Let's pull down into the area as if we hadn't seen a thing."

The kids were running along the shoreline, throwing rocks out into the water as we drove onto the causeway. Their father nonchalantly gave us a friendly nod as he began casting and retrieving in a more normal manner.

As I stepped out of the car, one of the youngsters bluntly inquired, "Who are you, and why have you got that gun?" It was obvious he was a rather friendly and inquisitive little tyke, a typical youngster—full of questions and demanding answers.

"I'm John, the local game warden," I responded. "What's your name?"

He never responded to my question, but inquired once again about the firearm on my gun belt. By then, the dad had joined us, directing the little fella to stop asking so many foolish questions.

"How are they biting?" I asked.

In a southern drawl, he said, "Ain't caught nothin' yet. Thought I'd bring the kids down here for a little somethin' to do."

I quickly glanced over at Jim with a slight grin on my face. The man was lying through his teeth, and he was some damn good at it. Never once did he exhibit any signs of the nervousness most liars show when confronted. If I hadn't just watched him hide the bass in the back of the van, I'd probably have taken him at his word, checked his fishing license, and left the area.

"Mind if I check your fishing license?" I asked politely. He obligingly removed it from his wallet and passed it to me. His name was Larry, and he came from nearby Knox Ridge.

"No luck at all, huh, Larry?" I asked again.

"Nope, not a thing," he stated. "The bass are spawning along the shoreline, but they won't bite. I guess you can't keep 'em this time of year anyways, can you?"

Aha! So Larry knew the rules . . . He was starting to dig himself a bigger hole—one that he might not be able to talk his way out of.

"Yeah," I said calmly, "the bass are on their beds right now. It would be pretty easy to snag one if a person tossed a lure directly onto their nests." Holding onto Larry's fishing license I said, "Larry, we want to make sure no one is snagging and possessing any of these bass. Why, just the other day I caught a fellow down here with three or four stashed in the trunk of his car. You wouldn't mind if we do a quick check of your vehicle, would you? We want to be sure and treat everyone the same."

"Oh, hell no—go right ahead," Larry said bravely, acting as if he was totally aboveboard and had nothing to hide. He quickly opened the back door of the van, displaying a pile of kids' toys and rolled-up blankets along with several other items not associated with fishing.

"See—nothing there!" he said, starting to close the door.

"I just want to take a quick look inside," I said as I climbed up into the body of the van. "Just want to be completely sure," I added. I searched through the blankets while slowly inching my way toward the spare tire.

"I hear ya!" Larry sputtered. "I ain't got nothin' to hide!"

With that, I lifted up the spare tire, exposing the still-wet bass. "Wow," I said. "What do we have here, Larry?"

By now, all of the kids were gathered around the van, watching the entire procedure.

"Well, I'll be gawd-damned!" Larry shouted. Without so much as batting an eyelash, he turned to the kids gathered at the rear of the van and began screaming, "Which one of you gawd-damned kids caught that fish and put it in here?" Shocked at being accused of doing something they hadn't done, the youngsters failed to respond to his belligerent demands.

I couldn't believe what I was witnessing. It was the worst act of cowardice I'd ever seen. Here was a grown man—a parent, no less—blaming his offspring for his own illegal activities. What kind of message was he sending to his kids?

Before Larry could intimidate these little tykes any more than he already had, I directed him to the solitude of my cruiser, where we could talk privately. Personally, I wanted to boot Larry squarely in the arse just as hard as I could. Any respect I might have had for him had disappeared in a flash. Disgusted, I said, "Larry, before you carry this little tirade any further, let me tell you something: We watched you snag that bass. We also watched you hide it in the van. How to hell do you think I knew where to find it, for God's sakes? I can't believe you've got the audacity to stand here accusing your own kids of doing something that you, yourself, have done. What kind of a man are you?"

Larry wasn't about to admit his sin. He adamantly stuck to his story—that one of those damn kids must have put the fish in there—

apparently not believing my explanation of how we'd watched him break the law. It was a senseless act in futility trying to discuss the issue any further with Larry, so I wrote out a summons charging him for the violation.

"I intend to fight this in every court I can. Matter of fact, I'll fight it all the way to the Supreme Court in Washington if I have to," Larry said arrogantly.

"That's your right, Larry. How about if we start in Belfast District Court, a week from Tuesday?" I said calmly as I continued writing out the court summons.

Fight it, Larry did; he requested a jury trial at a later date. It was a short trial, lasting only a few minutes, concluding with a guilty verdict handed down by his peers in record time, accompanied by a well-deserved tongue-lashing and a hefty fine from the disgruntled judge who had listened to Larry's pathetic testimony.

I departed the courthouse that day wondering what his family must have thought. Larry was certainly a sorry example of what parenting should be about. He became one of those memories that I'd just as soon have forgotten.

Halloween and the Unity Square Crapper

Halloween in Unity wouldn't have ever been the same without the traditional stolen outhouse being deposited in the middle of Main Street by a group of harmless pranksters having a little fun under the cover of darkness.

The stolen outhouse placed in town square was a highly anticipated annual tradition for a small group of local hoodlums.

Halloween of 1972 was no exception.

In addition to a crapper being placed in the middle of the road, there were the usual rolls of toilet paper hanging from the trees and the remains of shattered pumpkins scattered throughout town, all indications of the annual event.

On this particular night, a couple of college students and some local youths were engaged in a little egg-throwing battle just outside of town. It resulted in a rivalry that was close to getting totally out of hand.

This egg-throwing incident required a little extra police presence to reassure members of the public that their interests were being well protected.

Apparently during this egg-tossing melee, one of the college students got smacked upside the head by an egg that left a rather nasty bruise implanted upon his thick noggin. In turn, this student decided to rally a few cronies from the nearby college campus to settle the score with these local hoodlums running all over town, randomly tossing eggs at those who happened to venture within range of where they were hiding.

Anyone approaching their location was fair game, including law enforcement officers; more than once my cruiser was peppered with eggs as I slowly patrolled through the area.

Rumors began circulating around town of a pending brawl in front of the phone company, a small riot of sorts that was scheduled to occur shortly after dark in an effort to settle the score between the campus elite and the young townsfolk.

Maine State Police troopers Harry Bailey, Bob Bragg, James Young, and myself, along with several deputies from the Waldo County sheriff's office, were patrolling the area in a show of force just in case a need arose.

Sure enough, a large contingent of college students and local youths started gathering in the phone company parking lot as the early evening wore on. They were chanting and insulting each other, waiting to see who would start the brawl.

At this point, not all of these people were college students or local teenagers. There were quite a few older adults who rather anxiously had joined in on the action, apparently seeking a little excitement of their own.

Before those in the crowd got to the point of becoming totally uncontrollable, Trooper Bailey ordered them to immediately disperse, or they could expect a free one-way trip to the Waldo County Jail, compliments of their local law enforcement.

Harry had that intimidating demeanor that no one seemed to want to question. He obviously wasn't about to put up with any foolishness or compromising, as we stood shoulder to shoulder, ready to follow through on his promise if need be.

Reluctantly, the crowd decided not to push the issue, and what could have been a major fiasco wisely was averted.

Later that night after crawling into bed, thinking that all was finally quiet, I heard the drone of a car engine running outside my home. Peeking out through the window of my warden's camp window I observed a group of young men desperately trying to drag my own outhouse onto a trailer for the obvious trip over to Main Street in Unity.

Two of the outhouse thieves were none other than my tag-along partners of game warden wannabees, Gary and Jimmy, who obviously were hell-bent on having a little fun of their own.

Little did they know that stored inside the outhouse were several sticks of dynamite, explosives I used to remove beaver dams.

Certainly my outhouse and its explosive contents sitting in the middle of downtown Unity was not a very good choice. Especially if, as had happened in the past, the crapper—with more than a dozen sticks of dynamite inside it—was burnt or demolished by an errant vehicle before daylight.

I scampered out of the warden's camp in a wild rage, quickly discouraging their activities. I'm sure the boys had never seen me in a wild rage like that before, as I watched them hightail it back to their vehicle, quickly scurrying away from the area like wounded rabbits being chased by a mad hound.

The next morning I was awakened by the sounds of my wife blowing her car horn as she attempted to head off to work.

Looking out through the bedroom window, again I found the cause of this latest commotion to be someone else's outhouse neatly sitting in the middle of my driveway. It was a bright red, well-constructed, and neatly decorated outhouse.

I didn't know where it came from, but I certainly had a good idea of who brought it there!

Mrs. Ford couldn't leave the yard until I moved the crapper out of her way.

In the process of moving the outhouse, I buried my cruiser in a layer of mud on my lawn, the result of several days of heavy fall rains.

My next-door neighbor, observing my dilemma, generously offered his assistance. He slid into my dooryard with his farm tractor, hoping to pull my cruiser back onto solid ground.

Before we knew it, his tractor also became encased in the gooey mud of what was once my well-manicured lawn.

Now, not only did I have a brightly decorated outhouse that only God knew who it belonged to perched upon my lawn, but my cruiser was buried along one side of it, and a farm tractor was buried up to its axle in goo on the other side. My precious lawn was beginning to look like a country junkyard.

A quick call to Cliff Ham and his wrecker in Unity, along with an urgent plea for our rescue, found us spending the next two hours digging and hauling these mechanical beasts back onto solid ground.

I was loudly sputtering words that morning that I never knew existed. It was a damned good thing my young ride-along buddies didn't show up to see what was going on, because in the mood I was in, homicide wouldn't have been out of the question!

Eventually, I managed to pull the outhouse in behind the camp and out of the way. I still had no idea of where it came from until a few days later, when a camp owner from the nearby town of Pittsfield skidded into my dooryard, madder than a pit bull with rabies. He demanded, "What the hell are you doing with my outhouse parked in your backyard? You're supposed to be a gawd-damned law enforcement officer, and you've stolen my outhouse!" he angrily bellowed.

I was nearly a month of Sundays and two Saturdays trying to calm him down, as I desperately attempted to explain how his crapper just happened to be perched in my dooryard.

After allowing him to rant and rave rather freely, Gerald and I actually became the best of buddies that day. It was a hell of a way to gain a new friendship, especially through the theft of an outhouse, but that seemed to be the way things happened in this profession.

Even with the failed attempt at stealing my crapper, Unity didn't escape the 1972 Halloween night without someone else's outhouse being placed in the middle of the square.

From what I was told, one arrived in the middle of town during the wee hours of the morning— at a time when most decent folks were home in bed and sound asleep.

One of the young thieves involved in the caper decided he wanted to use the little house for what it was intended. As he was doing so, his buddies decided to have a little fun. They thought it would be fun to make a couple of quick passes with their truck just as close to the outhouse as they could get, while he was occupied inside the little building.

On their last run they accidentally collided with the structure, smashing it all to pieces, with Barry seated inside. Fortunately for Barry, he'd consumed just enough liquid spirits to protect him from any serious harm.

Other than a few bumps and bruises, he wasn't hurt.

I swear that young fellow was like a cat—he definitely had been blessed with nine lives. In the short time I'd gotten to know him, he'd used up at least eight of them.

The Flying Flashlight

In the early 1970s the Maine State Legislature passed legislation calling for stricter penalties for those found committing the act of night-hunting. This penalty change came about because the illegal activity seemed to be occurring at an alarming rate, with the precious deer herd paying the consequences.

The nighttime was extremely busy for most wardens covering central Maine. These new penalties resulted in a large number of bad hombres forfeiting a family-heirloom rifle handed down from Grandpa's generation long ago as a down payment to the State for their illegal deeds. Additionally, these poachers had to cough up $500 of hard-earned cash as a means of forced penitence for their sins, dollars to be funneled into the General Fund of the State's coffers.

For the first offense, these hoodlums would be required to relinquish their freedom for a minimum of three days' incarceration at the county crowbar hotel, with a longer sentence in store if it was a second- or third-time offense.

Apparently, the new mandatory penalties had yet to be brought to the attention of many of the old diehard poachers. The lenient penalties of the good old days, consisting of a mere slap on the wrist and a $200 fine, were long gone.

I was working night-hunters in my area one fall evening, accompanied by my working partner, Warden Doug Miner of Hampden, and my ride-along friend, Gary. It was cold and frosty with a bright harvest moon shining high overhead that occasionally became obscured by the dark clouds drifting in front of it. A little after midnight, we were advised of some night-hunting occurring in a large set of fields near the auction hall on Horseback Road in Burnham, a regular feeding ground for deer. The complainant had reportedly observed people in a vehicle illuminating these fields, located near his house, followed by two rifle shots. The complainant then watched a man exit the vehicle and run across the field, only to lose sight of him when the clouds covered the bright moon. The offending vehicle had quickly departed the scene at a high rate of speed, leading the caller to believe someone was still in the field, possibly recovering an illegally poached deer.

Normally, these types of complaints weren't worth following up on. By the time we were able to maneuver into the area undetected, the damage had already been done and the culprits were long gone. In this case, however, we were fairly close by; perhaps the odds might be a little more in our favor.

I said, "What the hell, Doug; it's pretty quiet tonight, and who knows—we might just get lucky."

"It's your district," Doug said. "You know it better than I do!" With his agreement we quickly headed for the scene.

There was no traffic on the road as I slowly cruised into a familiar hiding spot located within walking distance of where this activity was supposedly occurring. Quietly exiting the cruiser, we skirted along the edge of the road, heading for a vantage point where we could scan the field and search for any signs of human activity. It was colder outside than being in an open freezer in an igloo as we took cover among a small clump of pine trees situated along the edge of the large field.

The clouds that were covering the moon suddenly departed, and the bright moonlight flooded the entire field in front of us like a spotlight at a stage show. Some distance away, a man was slowly shuffling along the edge of the field, dragging something behind him. Something, like possibly a dead deer! Whenever a car cruised by, he immediately sought cover in the nearby woods, waiting until the vehicle had passed. He was still quite a distance away from our location, but it appeared as though he was headed our way.

I whispered to Doug and Gary, "We need to

remain perfectly still. Let him come to us before we make our presence known." It seemed like it took forever before this midnight hiker got within striking distance of where we were patiently waiting in the bushes. I found myself shivering almost uncontrollably—not so much from the cold, but from the anticipation of what was about to happen. It seemed as though the closer he came, the more traffic ventured into the area. Each time a vehicle approached, the man would dart back into the woods, emerging only after the car had traveled well away from the fields.

Finally, he was less than thirty yards away. It was show-and-tell time. The man was carrying a rifle in his arms and dragging a deer behind him, desperately struggling to accomplish this task. Hopefully he was tired enough so that his fight, or flight, would be very brief, at best.

I led the charge out from under the pine trees, screaming, "Game warden—hold it right there! You're under arrest!"

It was just like someone had poured raw turpentine on his bare butt. He immediately dropped the rifle and the deer and struck out across the field like a jackrabbit fleeing for his life. In a sense, that's exactly what he was doing. I was running a short distance behind him, with Gary and Doug bringing up the rear. He kept zigzagging back and forth, so as not to allow my outstretched hands the opportunity of snagging his scrawny little neck. The more I screamed for him to stop, the faster he seemed to run.

I was nearly out of breath and had gone just about as far as I could go when I yelled, "Put the lead to him! Put the lead to him!" thinking that perhaps this idle threat might convince him to surrender. He never had the chance to do so. Suddenly, a large solid object went sailing by my head and struck the fleeing man a solid blow right in the middle of his shoulder blades, knocking him head over teakettle into the damp grass. At that point, I could only fall on top of him, pin him to the ground, and wait for Doug and Gary to arrive to prevent him from escaping.

I made a serious attempt to read him his rights, but as I gasped for air, all I could muster was an exhausted, "You have the right . . . to . . . huh-huh-huh . . . remain . . . huh-huh-huh . . . silent. Anything you say . . ."

At that point Doug and Gary piled on top of us, reminding me of days gone by when I used to be on the bottom of the pig-pile in grammar school. One thing was for sure—no one was going anywhere!

I learned later that one of my partners (who shall remain nameless) thought I'd yelled, "Put the light to him! Put the light to him!" so he'd scaled his heavy metal flashlight at him like a skilled woodsman throwing a two-sided ax in an ax-throwing contest. He thought it just might slow him down a bit, and it certainly did.

Young Steve was none the worse for it all, other than being exhausted like the rest of us. Placing the metal bracelets around his wrist, we got ready for our long trip to Belfast. As we hiked back across the field, a car pulled up to the edge of the road, stopping just long enough to see what was going on. Blasting on the horn, the driver squealed away at a high rate of speed. This was undoubtedly the other culprit involved in the crime, but he was home-free, knowing damn well we couldn't identify him, and that his little buddy wasn't about to talk.

Steve's roommate, an older man nicknamed Marty, arrived at the jail shortly after we'd booked Steve for the criminal offense. The sheriff's dispatcher was quick to relay the message that Marty was highly agitated due to the night's events. Marty had made it quite clear to the jailers that I best not let my guard down, and that this matter wasn't about to be forgotten.

It was after three a.m. before I finally returned to the Burnham camp to crawl into bed, seeking some much-needed rest. Shortly afterward, I heard the sounds of a car's engine idling at the end of the driveway. Glancing out the bedroom window, I recognized the same vehicle that had pulled up to the edge of the field as we'd led Steve back to the cruiser.

Figuring that something drastic was about to happen—like the windows possibly being shot out of the camp, as they had been when Warden Thomas had dealt with a similar issue—I grabbed my loaded semiautomatic rifle and slowly slid the bedroom window open, ready to respond if need be. Wisely for them, better judgment prevailed; after a brief spell of being parked at the end of my driveway, they sped away with their tires squealing and the horn blaring.

The next day the scene at the courthouse was quite intense. The court officer had to step between Marty and me as the discussion grew quite heated about the previous night's activities. Although Marty made several idle threats, he knew just how far to push the issue without crossing the legal line of getting arrested. It wasn't a pretty sight. I figured I wouldn't be getting a Christmas card from Marty or Steve this year.

Steve was convicted of night-hunting after a jury trial in Superior Court a few months later. He claimed to have shot the deer earlier that day, deep in the woods, and that he'd gotten lost on his way out. Steve said he had been staggering around from dusk until midnight when we'd unexpectedly confronted him.

Disgustedly he sputtered, "I can't believe John thought I might have been night-hunting."

Apparently the jury didn't have a hard time

deciding the truth; he was found guilty of the charges in near-record time.

There was no doubt that these two characters were not above using violence and intimidation. This point became very evident a few years later when I and my deputy, game warden Scott Sienkiewicz, were the first responders at the scene of a fatal shooting in the town of Detroit in the dark of night. Steve had shot and killed Marty in what he claimed to have been self-defense. It was a very strange twist in a very strange relationship.

Steve was charged with manslaughter, but was acquitted of the crime. A witness testified that Marty was trying to attack Steve with a bayonet and that Steve did indeed shoot in self-defense.

Steve was much happier to see me on the night of the shooting than he'd been on the night I captured him in the field by the Burnham Auction Hall. I think he just wanted someone to talk to.

Taking the Plunge

One of our wintertime duties as game wardens was to check the area beaver flowages within our areas to make sure trappers were complying with regulations.

On a bitterly cold February morning in 1977, I headed off to check yet another one of those beaver ponds I'd located from the air while flying with my buddy Dana Toothaker the previous day. It was in an area I'd never been to before. As we circled low over the area it was obvious by the many set-poles surrounding the beaver house that several trappers had converged onto the frozen beaver pond. A few of these sets looked as if they might be a little closer to the beaver house than the twenty-five feet legally allowed by law. "There's a good place to snag a bad guy or two down there, John Boy," Dana had said as we scaled low over the treetops one more time in order to get a better view.

We'd experienced a rather hefty snowfall over the past few weeks, followed by an unusually warm February thaw. A few of those days had been so warm, it felt as though spring had arrived prematurely, but today there was no doubt winter was back in full force. The icy wind whistling through the trees with a light blanket of loose snow circling around in the frosty air was typical of a cold wintry day in the Northeast. The wind chill was dangerously below the freezing mark, nearly taking my breath away each time I inhaled. In a strange sort of way, it was quite peaceful and rewarding to be outside in the cold, performing my duties.

As I slowly hiked down through the thick woods, heading for the beaver flowage, I found myself wandering farther and farther away from my cruiser and civilization. I thought about the dramatic changes in climate over these past few days as I slowly shuffled along in the snow, my snowshoes holding me up on top of the deep snow. Suddenly I spooked a couple of whitetails who were snugly concealed beneath a grove of hemlock trees a short distance away from the path I had chosen. They crashed out through the woods in an effort to put as much distance between us as possible.

That's gratitude for you, I thought to myself. *I spend most of my career protecting these damn critters and they won't even hang around long enough for me to enjoy their beauty and grace. Oh well . . .*

I marched on through the woods, heading for the beaver flowage ahead. I was anxious to check out this new location. Had it not been for the earlier flight with my pal Dana, I never would have known of its existence, although the snowshoe trail that headed into the thick woods might have caught my attention sooner or later, as I patrolled through the area. The signs of snowshoe tracks heading into the woods often piqued my interest: Where did they lead, and for what purpose? More often than not these tracks would lead to situations where folks found themselves in trouble with the law.

Finally, I spotted the large beaver flowage a short distance ahead. A foggy mist was coming off the small stream flowing out of the beaver pond. The open water apparently was much warmer than the colder air, creating an eerie haze that was drifting down through the woods and the surrounding area. Thank God for my department parka and the wool uniform, protecting me from the extreme elements on days like this. With the hood pulled up high over my head, I was snug as a bug in a rug.

Carrying my faithful chisel, I was actually enjoying the trip as I trudged on through the light layer of snow that had fallen the previous night. Following the snowshoe tracks as best I could, I marched out onto the flowage and toward the many set-poles indicating where these beaver traps had been set. I finally reached my destination, better than a mile away from my cruiser. It was going to be an uphill walk back.

The huge beaver hut was completely surrounded by set-poles, indicating a large number of trappers who were seeking the furry inhabitants of the pond. As I walked among these poles, I noticed two of them were placed extremely close to the beaver house, well within what was deemed the restricted area by state regulations. Instead of the required minimum of twenty-five feet, these traps appeared to be less than eight feet away from the beaver house.

I immediately headed for them, intending to chop the ice away in order to seize the illegal sets. As I walked through the maze of poles where the majority of the traps were located, I suddenly found myself plunging down through the ice and into the icy cold water below. I was completely surrounded by the heavy spring-loaded traps attached to the set poles.

Everything happened so quickly. I instinctively extended my arms, catching myself on what little thin ice remained around me, still clutching the chisel in one hand. I was hanging midway up to my chest in the freezing water as I heard the ice cracking under the strain of my weight. For the time being the thin ice was preventing my shocked body from being completely submerged in the cold water. With snowshoes firmly attached to my feet, it would have been impossible to swim if I had to. I didn't dare to kick or thrash around, fearing one of the large 330 Conibear traps placed precariously close by might latch onto my snowshoes, or even worse, onto my foot. If that happened, I would be stuck there until some unsuspecting trapper showed up to check his traps, which could be days, if not weeks, later. The laws didn't require the beaver trapper to check his traps daily, as it did for other species.

Certain parts of my anatomy were signaling for me to get the hell out of there as fast as I could. My deep voice suddenly changed to a high soprano, if you know what I mean. I had serious doubts about whether I was going to survive this ice-cold dunking, especially weighted down by my wool pants and half-soaked heavy winter parka. I had no idea how deep this pond might be, and I didn't care to find out.

Somehow I managed to slowly inch myself back onto firmer footing, even as I heard the thin ice cracking all around me. To suddenly panic and start thrashing around could possibly result in a fatal ending. I decided I was too damn young for that to happen. Besides, I had a new son and a loving wife at home that I wanted to return to.

Finally I managed to roll up on top of ice that was a little more solid. I lay completely still for a minute, recouping my breath and strength. The cold wind and the swirling snow weren't helping matters any. That snug-as-a-bug-in-a-rug feeling no longer existed. Relieved to be back up on solid ice, I knew I had to get back to my cruiser real soon, or I might fall victim to the onslaught of hypothermia, a condition that claimed many lives each year. My heart was pounding like a jackhammer on a solid cement slab as I slowly stood up.

Within seconds my pants had turned into a solid layer of ice, making it extremely difficult to walk—and I had such a long way to go. I began following the trail back to my cruiser as quickly as I could, hoping that once I got back into the woods it wouldn't feel quite so cold. I was shivering uncontrollably, probably more from the excitement of my predicament than the cold temperatures encompassing me. Scurrying back up the narrow trail like a rabbit being chased by a possessive hound, I tried not to dillydally. I didn't bother stopping, not even for a rest, fearing if I did, I might not want to continue.

Along the way I saw those same two deer again; I swear they had smirks on their faces. This time they stood completely still, watching me drag my sorry tail past them. *I just might have to contact my old poaching buddy Grover to let him know where they were hanging out,* I thought as I scurried on by. *Go ahead and smirk at me, you damned thankless creatures.*

Finally off in the distance I could see my cruiser. It gave me a renewed burst of energy as I made my final big push forward. My wool trousers were frozen solid and felt like they were coated with a layer of iron. Every step was a chore, but finally I was unlocking the door of my cruiser and climbing inside. With a huge sigh of relief, I started the engine, turning the heater up high as I hastily shot down the narrow road, heading for a hot shower and some much-needed dry clothes. It wasn't very long before a blast of welcome heat from the car's heater was striking my face and thawing out my frozen body—just what the doctor ordered. I was grinning from ear to ear like a little kid with a brand-new toy, thankful to have survived yet another ordeal out in the wilderness.

Lights Out

I was spending yet another night away from home, trying to catch a desperado who was looking to blister a big buck underneath the beam of a bright spotlight. Faithful game warden wannabe Jim Ross and I had joined Warden Lowell Thomas to scout the Bog Road in Albion. It was the night before the opening of firearm season for deer, and if it was anything like what we'd seen in the past, we could be in for a busy one.

Jimmy had passed all the preliminaries of becoming a warden with flying colors. All that remained was the background check before he would be considered for future employment. It appeared as though Jim was well on his way to fulfilling his dream of becoming a game warden.

If anyone deserved this, it was Jim Ross. Ever since the day we'd experienced a chance meeting in 1971 out on the ice of Unity Pond, this young man had demonstrated his desire to become a Maine game warden many times over. He had volunteered countless hours to the cause, and had been personally involved in many Fish and Game cases. We had experienced some rather exciting times together, with Jimmy being involved in every aspect of what the warden's job entailed. He knew exactly what to expect if in fact he was to be hired.

Jim's enthusiasm was often a driving force that shamed me into working when my personal preference would have been to stay at home. Now it appeared as if my friend would soon have a district of his own. What a proud moment that would be.

On this night, we'd parked on a remote section of Bog Road in Albion, an area that had been experiencing some recent night-hunting activity. It was an extremely quiet night as we backed the cruiser into place. Located directly across the road from where we parked was a trail winding down through the woods that led to a huge set of fields planted with corn. As we snuggled into our hiding spot, the baying of a coon dog across the road disrupted the serenity of the night. Obviously someone was down in the cornfields, hunting coon.

State law allowed the hunting of raccoons during the nighttime, but only when hunters used a trained coon dog and possessed nothing more than a .22 caliber handgun. Coon hunting was an extremely popular sport, with a few hunters actually able to make a living by selling coon pelts to fur buyers at season's end. Most of these coon hunters were honorable and respectable sportsmen in pursuit of their quarry, but like everything else, there were some who used the pretext of coon hunting to hunt deer at the same time. Those folks needed to be closely watched.

As we sat in the car, chatting, we heard a series of pops off in the distance. It sounded as if they were shots from a small-caliber firearm, coming from the cornfields where the coon dog had been baying. After the shots there was dead silence, indicating that the hunt was probably over. Lowell said, "They'll be coming out through that old road across from us in a few minutes. We ought to check them, just to be sure they're on the up-and-up, and to let them know we're around."

Sure enough, within a few minutes the glow of approaching headlights lit the tops of the trees at the back of the field we were watching. The tote road exited onto the main road directly across from our location. Quickly, we ran from the cruiser to the intersection. Hiding in the thick bushes along the edge of the tote road, we patiently waited as the pickup truck slowly approached.

Figuring this stop would be no more than a routine check of a couple of good ol' boys and their dogs, out enjoying an evening together, we decided it wouldn't do any harm to check for loaded guns, licenses, and the likes, if for nothing more than to let them know we were around. When the truck was just a few feet away, Lowell said, "Okay, let's get 'em." We turned on our flashlights and stepped out in the roadway, signaling for them to stop.

The truck skidded to a halt, all right, but much to our surprise, standing in the open body of the vehicle was a man with a high-powered rifle leaning across the roof, ready to shoot a deer as soon as he saw one underneath their headlights. This particular group of coon hunters obviously needed that little extra watching.

The rifle-toting hunter quickly scaled the back of the truck with his rifle in hand, heading for the nearby woods at a dead run. I was hot on his heels, with Jimmy close behind. We kept yelling and demanding that he stop, but all to no avail. I was holding the beam of my flashlight directly on the back of his head as we hightailed it through the bushes and woods just as fast as our little legs would carry us.

I could see the rifle gripped tightly in the man's hands as he sprinted among the trees, banging and crashing into the brush along the way. All the while, I kept my beam of light aimed on the back of his head in order to see exactly what he was doing. Suddenly, it dawned on me: It was my beam of light that was allowing him to see where he was going. I quickly skidded to an abrupt stop, pointing my flashlight straight up in the air. Jimmy damn near bowled me over as he slid on the moist leaves to a sudden halt alongside me. We heard the brush breaking a short distance in front of us, followed by a god-awful, sickening thud and a loud crash, and then nothing but dead silence.

Jimmy and I found the man—I recognized him right away as Raymond, a routine violator—sprawled in a pile of brush, his loaded rifle beside him. He was extremely dazed, with a small amount of blood seeping from his nose and mouth. I quickly handcuffed Raymond and checked for any serious injuries, then patiently waited for him to regain his senses. I knew he had to be more alert before I tried to carry on an intelligent conversation with him, or march him back out of the woods to rejoin his buddies.

Ray kept muttering, "What happened? What happened?"

"It looks like it was lights out, Ray—lights out!" I said.

Ray smiled sheepishly, realizing exactly what I meant. "I'm gonna lose my rifle, ain't I, John?" he inquired rather pathetically.

"I'm afraid so, Ray."

Recently Ray and I had been through some official business with each other after he and a buddy had decided to shoot every one of a farmer's tame ducks next to the farmhouse where the old man lived.

Meanwhile, back at the vehicle, Lowell was detaining two highly inebriated hunters who were desperately trying to convince him that no one else had accompanied them. They couldn't seem to understand why Lowell was so upset.

It was no surprise to learn who these men were once we got the entire crew together. Like my old pal Grover, Harvey, the leader of the group, was another much-talked-about poacher in the area. This wasn't the first time these fellows had been in trouble with the law, and it surely wouldn't be the last.

A few weeks later these bandits requested a jury trial in Kennebec County Superior Court, after recruiting a well-known Waterville attorney who all but promised them they'd never be convicted of the night-hunting charges. It just so happened that by the time their trial was scheduled, Jimmy had joined the ranks, becoming one of Maine's newest game wardens. It was only his second day at warden school when he was subpoenaed to show up in Augusta Superior Court as a witness.

The defense attorney, upon seeing a young rookie warden who was actually in his early twenties, but looked like a teenager, cockily bragged to his clients that the case would be short-lived once he got this rookie on the witness stand. The noted attorney was confident that Jimmy's inexperience would be a weak point in the State's case. He was confident he could confuse and trip up this young warden during his testimony, thus creating a shadow of doubt in the minds of the twelve jurors hearing the case.

He was adamant that his clients would be acquitted. Little did he know that calling Jimmy as his first witness would be his biggest mistake. The first question he asked of the state's newest baby game warden was, "Now, Warden Ross, would you please tell this jury just how long you've been a game warden?" It was quite obvious that he hoped to establish the young warden's inexperience, making every effort to reveal Jimmy's nervousness as he testified in a court of law. Without any hesitation whatsoever, Jimmy proudly puffed up his chest, leaned over the witness stand, and, looking the jury straight in the eyes, said, "I've been a Maine game warden for twenty-four hours, sir!"

The courtroom cracked up, as did the judge. It was a classic piece of testimony. This young warden, obviously proud of his new career, had overwhelmingly won over the jurors' hearts on the very first question asked of him. You could see the mood swing among the jury; they absolutely loved him. Jim was completely flawless during the rest of his testimony, obviously a big disappointment to the defense attorney.

It was a speedy verdict. After only a few minutes of deliberation, the jury found Raymond, Harvey, and Alan guilty of all charges. When darkness arrived later that evening, it was once again lights out for these bandits—only this time, inside Kennebec County Jail.

Mama, Mama, They've Had Babies!

There was one thing about being a law enforcement officer in my area: There never seemed to be an end to the practical jokes played between the agencies and officers. Most of the pranks we played were completely harmless, but they were always humorous. We were a family of brothers in uniform and friends of the best kind. We never knew from one minute to the next what to expect, but whenever the chips were down and one of us needed help, the others were always available.

Walter Chapin, a Maine state trooper, and his wife Madeline, along with their two children, Missy and Wally, lived in a trailer park in Unity. We were the best of friends. Walter's young-uns were of a magical age, just beginning to understand the big world around them.

One cool spring night as I was preparing to go to Bither Brook in Unity to work the annual smelt run, already under way, Walter asked if he could come along. I said sure; it was his night off, and I always welcomed a little company.

Normally the State Police were not noted for their patience, especially during long dark nights of surveillance. So it was that I informed Walter we'd be sneaking around in the chilly dark night for quite a while, and that he might get bored. I just wanted him to be well aware of this fact before he joined me for the evening. (In other words, if he came with me, he was along for the entire ride, and not just until he was ready to go.) He assured me that he was up for it.

Before we left that evening Walter's children begged us to catch a few live smelts to place in the small plastic swimming pool that they'd recently installed alongside their trailer.

"Daddy, maybe they'll have their babies in our pool!" young Missy said breathlessly,

Walter and I just chuckled.

The fish were running extremely well that evening, so I asked a friend to deposit a half-dozen of the six-inch smelts in a bucket of water to place in Walter's swimming pool, just as we'd promised Missy we would.

The Unity Pond smelts were much larger than any of the smelts from the neighboring ponds. Randall Pond in Brooks, for instance, actually had a run of smelts that were less than half the size of the Unity Pond smelts.

I dropped Walter off at home early that evening and we quickly deposited the live smelts into his swimming pool. His daughter was still awake, and anxiously watched the half-dozen fish as they darted around the edges of her swimming pool.

"Do you think they'll have babies, Daddy?" she asked.

"Probably they will at some point, dear, but we don't know for sure," Walter replied.

The kids were ecstatic at having their own smelt pond, with Missy thoroughly convinced there would be babies in the pool soon. I remember joking with Walter as I left their dooryard, saying, "Now, make sure those little critters don't have their babies too soon; you might find yourself over your limit!"

On the way home I decided to swing over to Randall Pond to check on that site's smelt run. Over the past few nights they had yet to make their charge up the small tributaries along the edge of the pond, but it was about time for them to once again perform Mother Nature's ritual, as they had done so many times before. Much to my surprise, on this night they were running. The small streams were black with the little fish as they swam in the swift current, depositing their eggs along the rocky bottom of the creek.

The few fishermen there were having great success in catching their legal limit of the small silvery critters. I convinced another friend to dip a mess of the small fish for me to keep in a pail of fresh water. I told him I had a special home for them, one that would make a little girl quite happy. Without questioning me further, he obliged. With a few dips of his fish net, I had several dozen small, lively smelts darting about in a pail of water.

It was the wee hours of the morning as I left Randall Pond, once again heading back to Unity. I was on a mission! I slowly crept into the small trailer park where the Chapins lived, armed with my bucket of live smelts. I dumped them into the swimming pool where Walter and I had placed the larger smelts a few hours earlier. My task completed, I quietly snuck away with a large grin on my face, wondering what the family's reaction would be in the morning.

Early the next day my phone was ringing off the hook. Walter was as excited as I'd ever heard him before; even sharing a few battles with drunken brawlers and domestic fights alongside my trooper buddy, I'd never known him to be quite this animated. I could hear his wife Madeline shouting in the background: "I don't believe this! I just don't believe it!" She was also in a mild state of hysteria.

"You ain't gonna believe this, John, but those damn smelts we dumped in the pool last night have had their young ones!" he shouted into the phone. "We've got a whole damn school of them in the pool, and the kids are going bananas!" It was quite obvious the entire Chapin family was on cloud nine, thoroughly convinced their six Unity Pond smelts had overnight produced a mighty miracle within their small swimming pool.

Walter continued speaking. "Missy came charging into our bedroom this morning, screaming, 'Daddy! Daddy! They've had their babies! The fish have had their babies! The swimming pool is right full of them!' " Walter had figured the fish we'd placed there the night before somehow looked bigger in the daylight hours, so he didn't put much stock in what his daughter was telling him. But upon her insistence, he slowly waddled outside to take a look for himself. "By God, John, that damn pool is alive with smelts! They've had their young!"

Walter, who knew as much about wildlife as what I knew about his job, was thoroughly convinced that the smelts had given birth in his swimming pool. I never let on as to what I'd done. I figured I'd let Walter and his family find out the truth for themselves later on; in the interim, they were all quite content with the way things had gone.

A few weeks later I received a radio call from my trooper buddy, asking to meet up with me in town. I could see a silly smirk on his face as I pulled up alongside his cruiser.

"You son of a gun! You put those extra little smelts in our pool that night, didn't you?" he asked.

I just looked at him and grinned. "Me! Walter, are you accusing me of doing something sneaky like that?"

The look on his face was priceless. "I knew it! I knew those damn fish wouldn't have their young in the pool! I knew it all along!" he said, trying to convince me. But in reality, my friend Walter hadn't had a clue. I never did find out who it was that set him straight, but I sure would have loved to have been there to witness it.

It was a long road with no turns in it, and I was sure that somewhere down that road I'd have my due coming. But for now, the warden had outwitted the trooper, which was right and proper.

Ralph's Biggest Buck

I'm sure that November day in 1978 started off like any other day for Ralph of Waterville. In an interview I conducted with him later that eventful day, he anxiously talked about how he had looked forward to participating in the deer-hunting season. Ralph admitted that he was a novice at the sport, but for quite some time had anxiously been anticipating taking part in the annual ritual. Ralph had hunted many years ago, but had only recently decided to seriously take up hunting once again at the age of forty-five.

For the past several years, the timing hadn't been right for him to enjoy the sport. It was a different story in 1978, however. Ralph was retired, and suddenly found he had far more time on his hands than ever before. It was time to catch up on experiences he'd missed.

To prepare for the big event, Ralph had studied several techniques in hopes of bagging a deer; he especially wanted to claim the prize of a big old buck to show off to his family and friends. One technique gaining in popularity throughout the country involved antler rubbing, a means of attempting to lure a buck into your rifle sights by making the critter think that another buck had invaded its sacred territory. Ralph had invested in all of the proper equipment to accomplish his quest of getting a big deer.

On this particular day, Ralph decided to hunt in the thick woods located on Unity Plantation, an area well noted for its large number of deer, especially the big bucks Ralph was seeking. It was a typical cool and frosty November day, when, in the early afternoon, Ralph found a place to park his truck. He headed out into the thick woods where he hoped to initiate his game plan. With rifle in hand and two sets of antlers, he trudged out through the brush following a partially grown-up logging road situated well away from the highway.

Eventually, Ralph came into a small clearing surrounded by dense brush. Deer tracks were everywhere, indicating it was a good place to set up shop. Tucking himself off to the side of the clearing, Ralph began rubbing the antlers together, using the method shown in the videos he'd watched. For a while, Ralph's efforts went unanswered and frustration soon settled in. Then, suddenly, there was a crashing of twigs and brush off to his north side. Something was definitely headed his way.

Ralph stopped rubbing the antlers and had his firearm in the ready position when and if the critter hiding off in the nearby brush came within range. His heart pounded as adrenaline flowed through his veins like never before. Then it grew silent again. Ralph slowly put down his rifle, picked up the antlers, and began rubbing them together once more, just as the videos had instructed him to do. As had happened before, the brush crashed and the ground crunched when something began rushing his way. This time, Ralph caught a glimpse of the creature's side as it swung just inside of the thick brush, running adjacent to the opening that he was watching. And once again, there was nothing but silence. This time, Ralph knew the animal was much closer than it had been before.

Slowly, Ralph picked up the antlers and made the grinding noise. By then it was nearing dusk but still well within legal hunting time. This time a large animal came bounding out from the nearby brush and into the clearing, right in front of Ralph. He was ready. He methodically aimed his rifle at the beast standing broadside to him. *Bam! Bam!* The mortally wounded animal ran a short distance back into the thick bushes before falling to the ground, dead.

Ralph excitedly ran to the spot where he found what he believed to be the biggest buck Maine had ever seen. Its rack was huge! His heart was pounding. He realized there was no way in hell he could haul this monster out of the woods all by himself. It was time to get help, and who better to call under these circumstances than the area game wardens. Surely, they'd want to see this monster buck, and maybe they'd help him secure it. Meanwhile, a short distance away, I'd met up with my sergeant in the parking lot of the Unity Phone Company. We were discussing our plans to work the area that night, along with other matters relating to the job.

Ralph quickly made his way back to the road where he flagged down a passing motorist who happened to be heading for Unity.

"I need you to do me a favor," he asked of the startled motorist. "I've just shot the biggest buck that Maine has ever seen, and I need help getting it out of the woods. It's too damn big for me to do it by myself. Will you call the Warden Service for me and see if they'll dispatch a game warden to come help? I'll wait here by my truck for them to show up," he said.

The motorist was headed to the pay phones in Unity when he spotted Bill and I parked in the phone company lot. He quickly pulled up beside us and relayed the message from the excited hunter patiently waiting a short distance down the road. Disgustedly, I said to Bill, "Jeezus, man—now we have to go help these hunters drag their damned old deer out of the woods? I hope this isn't going become a habit, or, worse yet, another permanent part of the job!" I was always finding something to gripe about regarding the many new tasks forced upon the wardens year after year. Besides that, like many of my counterparts, I simply liked to gripe. Still, my curiosity had me somewhat anticipating the short ride down the Waterville road to where the hunter was waiting. I also reasoned that if he needed a hand, it was probably better giving it to him now than finding him bottom end up in the brush, suffering from a heart attack because he wasn't physically in shape to begin with.

A few minutes later, Bill and I pulled up alongside a very excited Ralph as he patiently leaned up against his truck, hoping we'd respond.

"Boys, am I some damn glad to see you! You ain't gonna believe the big buck I've shot out there in the woods. I really doubt if the three of us will be able to haul it out," he said anxiously. "It's huge. I called it in with my antlers," he bragged.

Together, we hiked down the old logging road to where Ralph claimed his huge deer had fallen. By then, it was dark enough to require the use of our flashlights. We entered the small clearing where Ralph had been hunting.

"It's right over here," he said. By now he was all but running to where his trophy buck was located.

I was still grumbling to Bill. "The last thing I want to get into the habit of doing is hauling out a deer because hunters aren't capable of doing it themselves," I said. I was pretty sure he felt the same way as we shared a disgusted look between us.

"Here it is," Ralph hollered. He was ecstatic—as excited as any sportsman who'd just caught his first big fish, or shot his first partridge, or bagged his first big deer. Bill and I slowly wandered over, expecting to perhaps find an eight- or ten-point buck, which would've been normal for the area. Much to our surprise, lying there before us was a large brown carcass easily weighing five to six hundred pounds.

Ralph was correct. It had a real nice set of antlers, all right, but there was one slight problem: Sprawled out on the ground before us was the carcass of a medium-size bull moose. Bill and I looked at each other, rolling our eyes in disbelief. Either Ralph was trying to pull a fast one on us, or he really didn't have a clue what he'd shot. Looking at his face, it appeared to be the latter.

"Ralph, did you shoot this?" I asked calmly.

"Well, yeah—who do ya think shot it?"

"I think we've got a problem here, Ralph," Bill said.

"What do you mean?" Ralph asked, the look of ecstasy starting to vanish from his face.

"Ralph, do you honestly believe that's a buck?" I asked.

"Of course it is; otherwise, why would I have called you guys?" he mumbled pathetically. He was totally convinced he'd shot a deer.

"Yeah, there's a real problem, Ralph," Bill said. "You've shot a moose, not a deer!"

Ralph nearly fell to the ground as his hopes of becoming a statewide titleholder for the biggest buck Maine had ever seen were quickly dashed.

The next few minutes were rather pitiful as reality finally hit Ralph. Suddenly, he knew he was in a heap of trouble. Killing a moose was the most serious offense on the books for Fish and Game violations. Ralph had made a grave error.

I gathered Ralph's license and information, calmly informing him that we had no other choice but to take him to court for his actions. Even though it may have been an honest mistake, it was his responsibility to know his target and the type of game he was killing. I wondered how many other hunters just like Ralph were poking around in the woods.

Bill and I were somewhat sympathetic. It was tough to see a man who'd been so excited and exuberant about his accomplishment suddenly have the rug pulled out from under him, and then face a possible jail sentence and a large fine to boot. Ralph was devastated, to say the least, but he was humble and willing to accept total responsibility for his mistake, which although horrendous, had been an honest (if careless) action. He was cooperative with us in every way as we made arrangements to get the large moose hauled out of the woods with the aid of a local farmer and his skidder. Ralph willingly signed a voluntary statement describing his day and the events leading up to his mistake.

At Ralph's court hearing, I informed the judge of the circumstances, adding a word of support, recognizing and somewhat praising Ralph for his cooperation and honesty. Thankfully for Ralph, the judge showed real compassion, which he had the liberty to do. Ralph was assessed the normal fine, all of it suspended, although he was ordered to pay a $100 fee for court costs.

I'm sure Ralph's memory, of the "biggest buck Maine had ever seen," is still quite fresh in his mind today. I know it surely is in mine.

Confronting a Ghost

In October of 1979, I actually thought I was face-to-face with a ghost.

Two Unity College students had decided to go bird hunting behind a friend's house in Unity. Their friend Tom lived in the old farmhouse located off Quaker Hill Road. Tom had dropped out of school earlier that year due to personal issues. He was noted for his hard-partying lifestyle and illicit drug use, activities that would eventually lead to his downfall. According to his buddies, Tom would occasionally poach a deer behind the secluded farmhouse in order to put a little meat on the table. Tom's finances were in such disarray since quitting school that he had to take a deer every now and then just to survive.

We'd been experiencing what us Mainers call an Indian summer, with temperatures ranging from the mid- to upper 70s, or higher. It was an unusual spell of warm weather for this late in the fall.

As these two students walked through Tom's dooryard, they talked about not seeing him around for a while. They simply assumed he'd ventured off to visit friends elsewhere, as he so often did. As they passed a tar-papered shed near the rear of the farmhouse they got a strong whiff of a foul-smelling odor. They thought Tom might

...ve shot another deer that he hadn't take ca
...f, so they slowly ventured over to th li
...ilapidated shed for a closer look. a

They got the shock of their lives when g
peeked inside and found the lifeless remai c
Tom perched atop an old refrigerator. An e i
bottle of vodka and several pills were scatt
beside his lifeless body, with a large n
secured tightly around his neck. It appeared t
a suicide—the final ending for a young man v
could no longer deal with the pressures of life.

The two students called the Warden Servi
and I arrived a short time later. I comforted the
as best I could while we anxiously awaited th
arrival of the Maine State Police, who wou
investigate and handle the horrific scene insi
the small outbuilding. It was obvious Tom h
been there for a while, and that the warm weat
had aided in the rapid decaying process.

As soon as the troopers arrived and
customary investigative statements were ta
from the young men, they placed as much dist
as they could between themselves and the
farmhouse. I couldn't say that I blamed them
would be a day they'd remember for a long

I spent the better part of the day assistir t
trooper friends at the scene as they too d
photos and conducted their lengthy inv b
tion. I reflected on what I knew about Tom. so
met him in the past in my law enfo an

pacity. He had appeared to be an [...] [...] kable chap, very sociable and non [...] though his views on society—and on [...] eneral—left a lot to be desired. Tom [...] efinitely living in his own world, one that [...] nfluenced by drugs and alcohol, and nothi[...] vas about to change it. Nothing except death [...] —hat is.

Tom's family in New Hampshire was made aware of the untimely death of their loved one. The undertakers eventually arrived, performing the gruesome task of removing the badly decomposed body. The area was scoured for any signs of foul play, and finally, completely secured by those of us who had been at the site for most of the day.

I was still thinking about Tom as I finished patrolling that day. It was so sad to see a young ife wasted. I couldn't help but wonder if perhaps here was something I could have done to revent such a tragedy, even though I knew deep own there wasn't.

few days later, my legislative pal, Representa-ve Babe Tozier, was riding along with me for e afternoon. We were cruising around the strict, looking for some sort of trouble to get in, t overall it was a quiet day. It was nice to have neone along to shoot the breeze with. Babe I I always found something to talk about; if it

wasn't politics, it was some other unimportant topic that usually resulted in a chuckle or two between us.

As we cruised the area Babe inquired, "Fordy, where did that young fellow commit suicide a few days ago?"

I started to tell him, and then I said, "What the hell . . . We're only a little ways from there— I'll show you."

We headed for the old farmhouse, pulling into the narrow driveway a few minutes later. We slowly passed the old farmhouse and drove toward the spot where the little shed had been situated. Surprisingly, the small building had recently been torn down. There was nothing left but a pile of rubble on the ground.

"I'll be damned," I said to Babe. "Someone's torn the shed down, but it happened right where that pile of rubble is now." I pointed to the pile of old boards and tar paper, all that remained of the outbuilding.

We looked around the area. It appeared as though no one had been around the old farm-house since that fateful day when the dooryard was filled with police cruisers. The grass around the farm was tall and unkempt, and the mud surrounding the puddles in the driveway gave no indication of traffic having been in or out of the area. It looked exactly as it had when I was there a few days before. But obviously someone had been to the property, and had intentionally destroyed the shed.

Having seen enough, I backed the cruiser around and was heading past the farmhouse toward the highway when Babe said, "Fordy, I just saw someone looking out the upstairs window of the house!"

I said, "Yeah, right, Babe," and kept driving, thinking that he was pulling one of the pranks he was so noted for.

"No, Fordy, honestly, I did! There was someone looking out through the upstairs window of the farmhouse," he insisted.

Not knowing if anyone should really be there or not, I stopped the cruiser and slowly got out. I walked up to the front door and began knocking. I wasn't thoroughly convinced that Babe wasn't playing a joke, but in any case, felt compelled to check it out. I knocked on the door two or three times without a response. I glanced around to see if Babe was chuckling, once again wondering if he was playing another one of his pranks, when suddenly the door swung open.

I found myself standing face-to-face with a young man who was the spitting image of the deceased Tom. Had I not known of Tom's demise a few days before, I'd swear I was confronting him once again in living person. Everything from this man's hairstyle and clothing on down to his strange demeanor was exactly like Tom. I could barely speak as my knees locked together like a pair of vise grips firmly hooked onto a stubborn bolt that I was trying to remove.

"Who . . . who . . . who are you?" I nervously stuttered. All the while I was thinking to myself, *Why the hell did I ever decide to come back to this damned forsaken place?*

Eventually I was able to determine that the young man standing in the doorway was Tom's identical twin brother, Tim. He had hitchhiked from New Hampshire and was going through his brother's personal belongings. He had no car, no extra clothing, nor did he bring any of the normal traveling essentials with him. Like Tom, Tim was a rather strange-acting critter himself. Who knew that Tom had a brother, let alone an identical twin? In all honesty, I seriously thought I was confronting a ghost! Until that moment, I had been a total nonbeliever in the supernatural, but I was starting to believe, big-time!

After a brief discussion with Tim, I was quick to put as much distance between myself and him as possible. What little conversation we shared on that doorstep was mostly one-way, with Tim doing most of the talking. Tim's main concern was what had happened to the rope that had caused his brother's demise; he wanted to know who had it now, and how he could get it.

I wondered if perhaps he wasn't thinking of following in his brother's footsteps. I stated that the Maine State Police was in charge of the investigation, and any inquiries he might have should be directed to them. The entire conversation with Tim was very brief and to the point. It was one of those chats which I was some damn glad to have come to an abrupt ending. I offered my sincere condolences to Tim and his family as I quickly scurried back to my cruiser.

"C'mon, Babe, we're getting to hell out of here," I said, as I got back in the cruiser and started down the narrow driveway just as fast as I dared to drive.

"What the hell was that all about, Fordy?" Babe asked. "You look like you've seen a ghost!" He snickered.

"I'm not sure but what I have, Babe!" I said, filling him in on the uneasy few minutes I'd just spent with Tim.

"Really!" Babe said after I'd finished my account. "Hee-hee-hee . . . Aren't you glad we came here today?" he said in that devious way that only Babe could.

"Not really!" I sputtered. We shot out of there like a bullet being fired from a handgun.

Even now, whenever I pass by that old abandoned farmhouse, my thoughts return to that moment in time when I honestly thought I had met a ghost.

The Kenduskeag River Travesty

July of 1978 was a typical hot summer month in the central Maine area. There was little activity throughout the district until July 11, when a strange phenomenon influenced the run of Atlantic salmon heading up the Penobscot River on their annual trek to replenish their stock.

Bangor wasn't within my patrol area, but an urgent call from the boss requested nearly every warden in the division to immediately head that way. We were told to report in civilian clothes, with only a couple of officers remaining in uniform.

For an unspecified time we'd be working a detail along the banks of the Kenduskeag River as it flowed on down into the Penobscot River, straight through the heart of Bangor.

The extremely hot weather, along with a major drop of water in the Penobscot River, had caused the salmon to change their normal route of travel. Instinctively they followed the flow of cooler waters, which under these circumstances led them out of the Penobscot River and into the Kenduskeag River. It was an extremely unusual situation.

The Penobscot River normally had the cooler temperatures and a steadier current, but this year there was a change. The power companies were holding back the flow of water at the dam further upstream. This condition consequently caused a dramatic change in the water temperature and the flow of water channeling downstream.

The current coming out of the Kenduskeag was much stronger and the water was somewhat cooler, thus causing the salmon in the river to migrate up the smaller tributary stream instead of following their normal route of travel in the open Penobscot River.

During the periods of low tide these conditions left many large salmon landlocked in dead pools of tidal water, helplessly awaiting the arrival of high tide once again before they could migrate back to freedom.

In other words, they were trapped for a six-hour period without any means of escape.

These salmon were huge in size, ranging from three to fifteen pounds or larger, and twenty to thirty inches in length.

In many of these tidal pools there were dozens of salmon caught helplessly in the shallow tidal waters, waiting for the ocean to rise again before they'd be set free.

The word quickly spread throughout the Bangor area regarding this phenomenon, creating an almost circus-like atmosphere along the water's edge.

Fishermen began flocking to the region, trying to catch a salmon. A few of them were actually trying to do it legally, while most were simply attempting to snag, or in some cases spear, these trapped fish. The entire fiasco was turning into a mass slaughter of one of the state's most prized fisheries.

The department was alerted to this injustice by several members of the local salmon club who were desperately trying to protect the return of the mighty salmon as they appeared in large numbers stranded within these landlocked tidal pools.

Standing along the parking lot adjacent to where the Kenduskeag River flowed through the middle of Bangor, it was nothing to observe schools of large salmon slowly making their way upstream during high tide, only to find themselves at the mercy of the elements once the tide turned and the waters lowered.

Wardens were strategically posted along the banks of the river, closely observing the many folks who'd gathered to witness this rather unusual event.

The department didn't want to make an large presentation of uniformed personnel making it look like overkill, but the temptation for snagging and illegally killing these big fish was quite evident based on a few of the onlookers who couldn't resist the temptation.

Fishermen with fly rods were anxiously hoping to entice one of these large fish into striking at the many flies being cast into the shallow pools, with little success, I might add.

As time passed, many more anglers arrived on the scene equipped with spinning rods and large treble hook lures.

Coached by friends and a few members of the public, they began casting their lures into the waters, slowly dragging the large metal hooks toward the salmon lying helplessly on the bottom of the pools. As the hooks bumped up against a fish, they'd yank the line, driving the sharp treble hooks into whatever part of the salmon these hooks touched.

The excitement would be on, as the salmon shot through the shallow waters, desperately trying to escape danger.

The crowd would hoop and holler, cheering on the angler who was committing such an atrocity.

Snagging fish in this manner is highly illegal, to say the least, but in order to prove the offense a warden had to witness the act, which unfortunately wouldn't have been accomplished if he was seen standing there in a uniform.

Several salmon had already been snagged in this manner, as evidenced on the return trip back to the ocean after the tidal waters had returned, freeing them from the small pools where they'd been trapped.

Large open wounds were visible on many of these fish as they migrated back out into the deeper waters. Some of them still had a fishing lure or two dangling from their sides, heads, and tails, indicating that they'd broken the line of those fishermen who were trying to snag them.

Many of these large fish would never recover from the horrendous injuries inflicted upon them. Instead they'd return back out to sea to die.

It was a travesty, to say the least.

As the hours passed and the days lingered, this fiasco became worse, and much more barbaric.

During the nighttime hours of low tide, people were sneaking along the banks of the small river with spears and pitchforks, slaughtering as many of the big fish as they could. Some were doing it simply for the kill, while others were actually pursuing a salmon to eat.

In one instance, a young man was actually swapping his illegally captured salmon at a local bar for free drinks. Rather humorously, the third time he snagged one, he was chased through a local department store by warden Doug Tibbetts and his partner as he fled the scene with his squirming salmon in his hands and the wardens close on his heels. He'd been apprehended twice before, only to be released on bail to recommit the crime again and again.

The patrons within the department store were screaming in panic as he shot out the door and eventually was tackled along Main Street by yet more wardens, as a fresh salmon went flopping and skidding down the sidewalk.

He was quickly whisked away to appear before a sitting judge who had seen his sorry mug a few days before. This time the judge sternly advised him, "Young fellow, I'm going to make this perfectly clear to you this time: Those salmon are going to be safe from you from now on, because I'm remanding you to the county jail. You are going to stay there until such time as every one of those damn salmon have returned out into the river where they belong."

With that being said, this young bar patron suddenly found himself perched behind bars, instead of sitting at one. Those of us in law enforcement viewed such a sentence as quick and poetic justice!

Many of the wardens in the division were asked to work long hours, as for more than a week this scenario repeated itself with each change of the tides. With each change of the tide came another influx of hoodlums, trying to outwit the fish cops hiding and patrolling the area. Those who were still attempting to capture a salmon caught in the tidal pools were a bit more skeptical of anyone watching them, but still they'd try.

In order to be close to the crime, some wardens, such as Warden Terry Glatt, stood at the pools in plainclothes with their own fishing gear, pretending to be fishing, while intently monitoring the activities of those around them.

I can't imagine what it would have been like

had not the forces shown up to protect these sea creatures from total destruction.

Wardens worked in teams, some of them walked the shoreline, watching and observing the activities of the crowds, while others were in uniform, parked in cruisers nearby, ready to spring into action if an undercover warden needed to corral someone for a violation.

Being dead tired and half-foolish from working the long hours we'd been putting in didn't help the situation any. It was a sure sign of fatigue.

During the night we were aided by the use of night-vision spotting scopes, allowing us to apprehend more than one poacher with a spear or pitchfork in their hands, trying to sneak into a small tidal pool harboring a salmon or two.

I spent more than one entire shift in the dark of night perched high upon the roof of a small shopping mall with a good view of the river winding along behind it.

Those with a devious mind assumed that three or four o'clock in the morning would be a good time to commit their dastardly deeds without being harassed by a damned old game warden.

Eventually the water temperatures and the flow returned back to normal, the salmon moved back into the main river where they belonged, and this brutal slaughter of one of the state's most cherished resources ended.

This was the only time during my warden's

career when these unusual conditions presented themselves in such a way. It was a time when I was ashamed of those people who seemed to care less whether these fish ever returned to this area year after year, or not.

Professional Courtesy, My Foot!

One sunny, warm day in late June of 1978, I decided to cruise down a narrow camp road leading out to an island at the far end of Unity Pond.

It was an area where the stream originating at Carlton Bog in Troy slowly flowed down through the countryside, eventually emptying into Unity Pond. It was a perfect place to catch a few perch, pickerel, and, more so, a good-size bass, especially this time of year.

As I pulled into the area, I noticed a New York vehicle parked alongside the narrow camp road. There was a man standing on the wooden-planked bridge, slowly casting and retrieving a lure from the stream. He was completely unaware of my approach.

When he finally noticed the cruiser heading his way, he tucked the fishing pole firmly underneath his arm and fled to the island like a track star trying to set a world record.

Aha, I thought, *another person without a fishing license,* and I quickly brought the cruiser to a screeching halt and chased after him, huffing and puffing all the way.

I knew any chance of him escaping was slim at

best, seeing as where his car was behind me, and he was stuck out on the scarcely wooded island.

He quickly spun off into what little thick brush there was as I hastily trotted in his direction.

At the location where he'd entered the woods, I noticed that firmly attached to a low-hanging branch was a red-and-white fishing lure with a trail of fishing line leading off into the pucker-brush.

What a great trail he had unwittingly left for me to follow! I simply traced the path of fishing line to a large hemlock tree with branches that hung low to the ground. Tucked underneath the backside of the tree, a man was lying motionless on the leaves.

He was obviously hoping I couldn't see him, although he stuck out like a fluorescent lightbulb in a darkened movie theater. He was sucked to the ground like a bedbug hugging a pillow.

I hollered, "Drop the fishing pole and come to hell out from underneath that tree," acting as though I was a soldier ready for hand-to-hand combat.

Sheepishly, the man crawled out from underneath the thick branches and slowly staggered in my direction. His arms were stretched off to his sides, reassuring me that he was not armed and dangerous.

"What the hell do you think you're doing?" I bluntly inquired.

"I ran because I didn't know who you were," he said. "I'm a cop too," he pathetically added.

"If you're a cop, what the hell are you running for?" I disgustedly demanded.

"I don't have a fishing license," he said.

"Gee, what a surprise," I said. "I'd never have guessed. Do you have any identification on you?"

The man quickly handed me a New York City Police Department ID card.

"Is this all you have?" I calmly asked.

"I've got my driver's license; will that do?" he nervously responded.

"Please—I'd like to see something a little more formal than your police ID," I stated.

"You're not going to write me a ticket, are you?" he asked.

"What the hell do you think I'm going to do?" I grumbled. "After going through those stupid shenanigans, don't you think you deserve it? I'd be damned if I'd tell someone I was a police officer after pulling a stunt like that," I said.

"Don't you guys know anything about professional courtesy?" he barked.

"Yes sir, I do! I know that professional courtesy is not running away from a fellow police officer," I sarcastically replied. "And you being a police officer, how to hell would you have felt had I done the same thing to you while you were performing your duties? Probably my sorry butt would have had a chunk of lead stuck in it.

"So to answer your question," I bellowed, "I *do* know about professional courtesy—and I'm going to extend it to you here today. Instead of hauling you off to jail like I really should, I'll give you the opportunity to take care of this through the mail. That way you can save yourself the humiliation of standing before a judge, trying to explain your sorry situation."

I was about as disgusted with this poor excuse of a police officer as with anyone I'd ever met. His attitude suddenly changed from being somewhat humble to becoming rather defiant and self-centered.

He was starting to infuriate me to the point where I was on the verge of hauling him off to the slammer just on the principle of it. Perhaps I should make him appear before the judge, to explain his defiance toward the laws of the land that he also took an oath to obey.

Fortunately for the man, whose name was Mark, he quickly realized he was about to get a free ride to the crowbar hotel as he pathetically begged for mercy.

"I'm sorry, Mark, but your attitude, along with the total disrespect you've shown to our profession, is a great concern to me. What makes you think you're any more above our laws than John Q. Public, who in normal circumstances would never have acted as stupidly as you've acted here today?" I bluntly asked.

Before giving him a chance to respond, I advised him that it might be in his best interest to take his summons, pay his fine, and move on, with perhaps a different attitude than what he was presenting; otherwise, he might find himself trying to make bail from the county lockup thirty miles away.

He wisely sensed my frustration and began grumbling to himself while impatiently waiting for his citation to court.

There was very little discussion between us as he quickly snatched the citation out of my hands and stormed away toward his vehicle, mumbling and grumbling to himself. I almost thought I caught a glimpse of that one-fingered salute that was still a sign of the times.

I can't believe how peaceful and relaxing this job could be one minute, and then in a matter of a few brief seconds, all hell would let loose and I'd find myself, once again, in the middle of a confrontation.

I guess that's why I'd always found this job to be so challenging and somewhat enjoyable. Dealing with the unknown always presents a challenge. Living on the edge, I guess you'd call it.

Not since the time I'd encountered another self-promoting culprit on Unity Pond—who presented me his Masonic membership card with a $20 bill attached to it as a means of identification, as I was about to write him a ticket—had I been so infuriated with my fellow man.

Not until today, that is.

That individual also came close to being arrested, for attempting to bribe an officer. But his pathetic insistence of it all being an honest mistake, while pretending not to have known the money was there, convinced me to do otherwise. Instead, I gave him the benefit of the doubt after finally obtaining his driver's license and making out the court summons.

I held onto the Masonic card while I completed the court documents.

"Can I have my Masonic card back?" he rather gruffly inquired.

"I'll give it back to you once I've copied the information from it. I want to notify your lodge of how you're using your sacred Masonic honor for your own personal needs," I said.

Needless to say, he became rather humbled and embarrassed as I handed him his paperwork, explaining how he could handle his legal obligations.

I never followed through with the threat to contact the lodge, but he never knew if I had or not. If nothing else, I hoped to teach him a lesson in humility.

Yup, dealing with my fellow man certainly can be quite challenging at times, especially when they find themselves in a precarious situation.

This New York City police officer was one of them.

I couldn't help but wonder what might happen if by some strange chance I ended up in New York City one day. I only hoped our paths would never cross.

A few days later, I was told that Mr. Cop made a special trip to Belfast to confer with the district attorney, as he tried to get the charges against him dropped on grounds of professional courtesy.

From what I was told, his reception there was no better than what it was when I yanked his sorry buns out from underneath that low-hanging hemlock branch along the shores of Unity Pond. It may have been even a little worse.

It was rewarding to know that fair and equal justice was alive and well in Waldo County.

Aided by Informants

It took a little time and effort, but eventually many of the local folks began to accept me as the game warden and the enforcer of the Fish and Game laws for their area. Trust was being developed, and along with that trust came a steady flow of information regarding people who were committing violations throughout the district. Happily, I was not only being paid by the public to do my job, but they were also willing to assist me in my efforts.

During the late summer and early fall of 1973, it was frequently reported that a few Burnhamites were illegally killing and selling deer to area folks and nonresident hunters from the surrounding countryside. These violators had actually sold a few of these dead critters to game wardens posing as nonresident hunters. An investigation was initiated when undercover detectives talked with various informants in the area and carefully dissected the information they received.

A few of the informants appeared genuinely concerned about the illegal activities they were reporting. Others were simply seeking revenge against someone with whom they had an ax to grind. For them, being able to get that person into trouble with the law would more than accomplish their goal. Then there were a select few who simply got a thrill by playing the role of a cop themselves, reporting an illegal activity to an officer and then watching as the culprits were held accountable.

There were even occasions when an informant provided information about people they knew, setting them up in hopes that the violator would get caught and they could witness it from afar. Sometimes, these informants were doing the same illegal things as the law-breaking individuals who they were reporting. It was a turf struggle of sorts—one person had staked claim to a territory, and anyone who invaded that territory was a threat.

For example, Arthur from Unity was loudly squawking about Dave from Troy taking more than his legal limit of smelts from the Bither Brook smelt run. Supposedly Dave was filling his containers with the legal two-quart limit of smelts, but also stuffing his chest-waders full of the small silvery fish. Dave openly bragged to his buddies about walking on past "that stupid game warden" with the illegal fish hidden in his waders. Arthur felt Dave was a might bit too brazen about his illegal activities, so he decided to squeal.

A few nights later I apprehended Dave as he

was nonchalantly hiking back to his vehicle. I asked to check his legal limit of smelts just as he was about to get into his car. He was extremely calm and cooperative until I asked him to drop his waders. My request to Dave amounted to a version of a smelt-brook strip search. The sweat began running down Dave's brow as he offered every excuse possible for not wanting to drop his waders. When he'd exhausted every option and slowly lowered the waders, sure enough, the small silvery fish were clinging from the top of his pants all the way down to his feet, putting him well over his legal limit.

"They must've fallen from my net and into my waders, John," he said sheepishly.

Grinning ever so coyly, I said, "Obviously they did, Dave! Obviously they did!"

As I wrote Dave up for the violation, he said, "John, can I tell you something about Arthur from Unity? He's taking way over his limit of fish almost every night, and he's bragging to everybody about it! He stashes hidden containers of smelts well away from the brook, planning to pick them up once he figures you've left the area and gone home to bed. Then he returns to the brook and starts dipping all over again! He's slaughtering the smelt population, John!"

Listening to Dave squeal on Arthur, I assured him I'd work on it. I shook my head in total disbelief as I walked back to my cruiser, thinking,

If you only knew, Dave . . . if you only knew!

A few nights later, I located Arthur's hidden containers of smelts at the end of the camp road, exactly where Dave had said they'd be. As Dave promised, Arthur arrived during the wee hours of the morning to retrieve his cache.

Needless to say, once the legalities were over, both Dave and Arthur continued chumming around together, and I was labeled the real bastard for holding them accountable. That was the way it was with some informants. Obviously, there had been a rivalry of sorts between these two over the years, and apparently I became the means of settling the score for both of them. In the end, while I knew that neither of them could ever be trusted, I also knew that their information was good!

In another incident, a young man from Kennebec County purchased an illegally harvested deer from a local Burnham poacher named Roger. The man paid for the critter with a personal check that lacked sufficient funds to cover the purchase. As a means of sending a message that deceitfulness among crooks wouldn't be tolerated, Roger kicked the crap out of the poor guy, sending him to the hospital.

Because of his severe injuries, I was called in to investigate the matter and to prosecute Roger. In this case, the victim confined to his hospital bed willingly became my informant, seeking revenge against Roger, who had pounded the hell out of him.

Once I confronted Roger with the somber facts and he pleaded guilty at a court hearing, he boasted, "It was worth every gawd-damned penny of the fine I was assessed, John. No one screws me and gets away with it."

Roger showed absolutely no remorse for what he'd done.

On another case, an informant desperately wanted to end his brother-in-law Ronny's illegal business of killing and selling deer. Obviously, there was no family loyalty between these two. The informant agreed to introduce an agent of the department, posing as a nonresident hunter, to his brother-in-law. They quickly secured a large buck for a minimal fee of $125. This deer had been shot underneath a light the night before, on the outskirts of Unity village.

After taking possession of the eight-pointer, we immediately obtained an arrest warrant for Ronny. Rounding him up the next day for the illegal violations, I charged him with illegally selling deer and for killing a whitetail after dark. The informant had remained nameless and well protected, both in the request for the arrest warrant and in the affidavit; however, a few nights (and drinks) later, my informant foolishly bragged about what he'd done. The end result was yet another thumping of the good guy by the bad guy, and another person sent off to the hospital. So much for family love! I could only imagine what their next family reunion would be like in the months following this melee.

In 1973, the local sporting camp near my Burnham residence was infiltrated by a couple of undercover wardens posing as nonresident hunters. At my request, they discovered just how illegal this sporting operation was. I'd developed a lengthy list of tips from several area informants regarding the illegal activities at this public sporting camp, which included illegal deer drives and many other daytime violations, along with paid night-hunting excursions down the Sebasticook River between Burnham and Clinton via canoe.

I'd suspected these folks of being dishonest for a long time, but proving it had been difficult. In the end, prove it we did, and then some. The camp was permanently closed and disbanded, and several employees who had previously guided for the owner were convicted of their illegal activities. Justice prevailed, and word rapidly spread throughout the area that the free rein enjoyed by these individuals had finally come to an end. Relying upon dependable informants to aid me in protecting the area's fish and wildlife resources was priceless.

Occasionally some violator would commit a heinous act that resulted in their best buddies turning them in because they were so offended by the illegal activity. Such was the case in the fall of 1973, when an informant advised me to go out behind his friend Phil's house in Troy, where I'd find an illegally set trap with something in it.

The trap itself was legal; the fact that it hadn't been tended to for several weeks was the violation he spoke of. Apparently a neighbor's dog had been caught in the iron-jawed device, where it died of starvation. Phil's total disregard of the trapping laws—laws that required each trap to be physically tended at least once every twenty-four hours—was quite obvious. The brutality and cruel death of this poor dog was a bit more than my informant could stand.

"That poor creature died a slow and miserable death," he said. "If only Phil had tended his sets like he should have, none of this would've happened."

Phil was ordered into court for the violation. I listened to every excuse in the world for why he couldn't check the trap. In this situation, no excuse was acceptable. I still shudder at the thought of how that poor dog must have suffered as he awaited the slow death he was subjected to. In this particular incident, the informant placed a civil obligation above friendship, and in doing so he may have prevented a similar situation from occurring in the future.

Every police officer depends upon a variety of informants from the public they serve during their careers. Without them, the job of a law enforcement officer would be extremely difficult and tedious. I find myself chuckling today as I look back upon some of the fiascos I often found myself involved in, thanks to the support of a community willing to assist me in carrying out those duties. Sometimes it became a guessing game, trying to figure out the individual motives of the informants, but all in all, without them, I wouldn't have had much of a career.

Being Mr. Nice Guy

There were times throughout my career when I found that people who were running up against a little hard luck could perhaps use some leniency rather than the heavy hand of the law to determine the outcome of some violation they may have committed. Fortunately I had the discretion to use my own judgment over whether to lower the boom on a violator or to extend a little compromise, knowing that it might be beneficial to the overall goals of my profession in the long run.

It really didn't matter which route I chose to take, just as long as whatever justice I meted out was being fairly administered to those I confronted.

A prime example of this involved a young man I found fishing at a secluded spot on Unity Pond in the spring of 1972. He was surrounded by his tribe of young kids, and they obviously were after a mess of white perch for fish chowder. I was well acquainted with this family and knew they were struggling financially, trying to make ends meet. Unfortunately on this day, Dad had failed to purchase a fishing license and was simply taking a chance that he wouldn't get caught.

Upon confronting him, he admitted his sins.

"I just didn't have the money to buy one, John!" he said. I knew that to charge him with the offense, I'd not only be severely penalizing him, but I'd also be taking away from the family. The end result would be far more detrimental to the well-being of the family than what justice normally required.

I said, "Tom, I can't simply ignore the fact that you've broken the law, nor can I treat you any different than anyone else, but I'll tell you what I will do. I'm going to give you a summons to court for fishing without a license, but I'm going to date it way ahead, for two months from now. Do you think that in the meantime you could save up enough money to buy your fishing license?"

"I think so," he replied.

"Well, here's the deal, Tom: You buy your license and you bring it to me as proof that you've met your legal obligation and I'll rip up this summons," I proposed. "We'll forget any of this ever happened. How's that sound?"

"You mean I won't have to go to court?" he asked.

"Not if you get your license and show it to me," I said. "That way you won't have to pay a hefty fine, the State will be happy, and I'll be happy."

"God, that would be great, John," Tom said gratefully. "I certainly can't afford any fine. I got all I can do to feed these little tykes now!"

"I know, I know," I said as we shook hands, securing the deal between us. I passed the written summons over to him. "Bring this along with your fishing license when you get it and we'll be all set," I said. "Otherwise, you'll have to show up in court on the day I've scheduled, and our little deal is off."

"Thank you, John!" He smiled. "You'll be seeing me real soon," he promised.

Two weeks later Tom showed up in my dooryard with a valid fishing license and his copy of the summons. I quickly discarded the court summons as I'd promised.

Tom then unexpectedly offered some vital information regarding a high-profile case I'd been working on since early November of 1970. This case involved a Thorndike hunter who had been shot through his arm, the bullet grazing his chest. He was left lying on the edge of the field for his buddy, who had been seated alongside of him, to deal with. One of the bullets had sailed between their heads, tossing bits of the broken branches into their eyes. The unknown shooter had quickly fled the scene, leaving a few articles of evidence behind, including the spent cartridges from the rifle he'd used, an old green hat, and a few clumps of human hair found firmly wedged in a broken branch just above where the hat had fallen to the ground.

With nothing but these few articles of physical

evidence to go on, and no suspect, this case had grown cold and remained unsolved. It was the only open hunting-accident investigation left within the state at that time. Every promising lead had seemed to come to a dead end.

Tom said, "John, you did me a big favor, and now I'm going to do you one."

"What's that?" I inquired.

"I'm going to tell you who shot that hunter in Thorndike a while back and just left him wounded in the field," he whispered. Tom then commenced to relate facts about the case that only myself and the other investigators had been privy to.

"You found an old green hat underneath a broken tree limb where this man fled the scene after the shooting, didn't you?" he asked.

I didn't answer him, but I'm sure it was rather obvious he had seriously sparked my interest. He then went on to say, "The shell casings you retrieved came from a .300 Savage rifle, and there were three of them, wasn't there?" So far, he was right on the mark. I felt my heart pounding as suddenly this cold case seemed within reach of finally being resolved.

Tom then named the person who he suspected of doing the shooting, along with a few other reasons for his belief. It all fell into place once I heard the name and considered the facts as Tom relayed them.

A few days later, Warden Safety Officer John Marsh and I contacted this newest suspect and confronted him with these recently obtained facts. Within a few brief minutes we had a signed and written confession from the man, confessing to his dastardly deed. He seemed to be quite relieved to no longer have to look over his shoulder, wondering when and if he might be arrested. His conscience had mentally done quite a number on him.

This case might never have been solved had it not been for the simple fact that I'd exercised a little leniency for a fishing-license case on Unity Pond. In this instance, being Mr. Nice Guy had paid big dividends.

Sometimes, though, taking such an approach didn't work so well. In August of 1972 Smalley Chandler and I had just apprehended a carload of young night-hunters in Burnham. They were toting a loaded twelve-gauge shotgun and illuminating the field with a bright spotlight in the wee hours of the morning. As they passed our location, flashing the bright light into the fields, searching for the eyes of a whitetail, it was obvious they were night-hunting.

We had draped a parachute over our vehicle to camouflage it, keeping the chrome and the windshield from shining if they happened to aim a light in our direction. Once they'd passed us, I exited the cruiser and quickly ripped the parachute off the hood and threw it to the ground. Jumping back into the cruiser, Smalley shot out into the darkness without headlights, quickly catching up to these offenders a short distance down the road. Making the stop, we immediately arrested this group of night-hunting banditos, informing them they'd be getting a free trip to the Waldo County Crowbar Hotel.

One of these subjects, who went by the name of JR, certainly wasn't the brightest candle on the birthday cake, but he wasn't a bad sort of chap either. I kind of liked him, simply because nothing ever seemed to bother him.

JR stated, "I got to go to the bathroom, John!" I remembered hearing that old excuse before, and I also remembered what the results had been when I had denied permission for the person to go. Obligingly, I took JR behind the cruiser so he could relieve himself. As he stood there doing his chore, he suddenly said, "What the hell is that thing you guys are dragging behind your cruiser?"

Flashing my light onto the ground I observed the parachute I thought I'd thrown well away from the car. Instead, it had become entangled into the back wheels and was firmly stuck in among the drive train of Smalley's cruiser.

JR said, "That's a gawd-damned parachute!"

As calmly and as seriously as I could, without laughing, I said, "Yup, JR, that's exactly what it is. We were going so damn fast to catch up with you guys that we had to use it to get stopped. You know, it's kinda like one of them dragsters at a race track. All of the warden cruisers are equipped with 'em now," I bragged.

"You gotta be shitting me!" Old JR shook his head in total amazement.

He couldn't wait to tell his cronies about the hot rod we had for a cruiser. "Them boys used a parachute to get stopped," he told his friends.

In a way, I felt sorry for JR. I knew his home was poorly outfitted, and he barely had the financial means to feed his family, but he still managed to find the money to buy a six-pack of beer and to be out raising hell with his buddies on a regular basis.

Being Mr. Nice Guy, I told JR that if he cared to swing by my place in the next day or so, I had a big box of nice dishes that he could have for his house. I wasn't really using them anymore, and they were his if he wanted them. JR seemed quite excited, and said he'd be over the next day, once he got bailed out of jail.

Sure enough, late the next afternoon JR came rolling into the yard in his beat-up old road-buggy, a vehicle that was barely street-legal (if in fact it even was). "You serious about those plates and dishes?" he asked. "My woman said she'd love to have them."

I retrieved the large cardboard box containing

several heavy dinner plates and some other dishes. "Thank ya, John Boy! Thank ya!" JR said, as he quickly backed out of the driveway, heading for home.

A few days later I happened to drive by JR's home while patrolling. I'll be damned if I didn't find him standing out behind the house sighting in his rifle. He was using the plates I'd given him earlier for a target. Now that's gratitude for you! It just goes to show that sometimes being Mr. Nice Guy pays off, and other times it makes little, if any, difference.

A Little Courtroom Humor

One of the tasks of my profession was dealing with the courts throughout our state, representing the department during pleas and arraignments as well as testifying under oath whenever needed. The majority of Fish and Game cases were usually heard before a judge at the district court level, but occasionally a defendant would request a jury trial in Superior Court in front of twelve of his peers.

It's amazing how slowly the judicial system functioned back then. Without exception, I always found that those who were running the outfit had a hurry-up-and-wait attitude. Unfortunately, this extremely slow process was the rule of thumb for our legal system in days gone by, and it's the same today!

I experienced some rather humorous incidents in the courtrooms of Waldo County. One thing is for certain: There was no way of predicting what a day in court might bring.

Coming out of the Closet

My very first official assignment at the Belfast District Court was to represent the Fish and Game Department at the 9 a.m. arraignments.

Being new at the job and rather unfamiliar with the expected procedure and the folks running the show at the courthouse, I decided to get a little earlier start when I left the Burnham warden's camp that morning. Thank God I did!

I had polished my boots, shined my leather gear, and crawled into a newly pressed uniform, hoping to make a lasting impression upon those I'd be dealing with that day. Arriving at the courthouse quite early, I enthusiastically jumped out of my cruiser and was headed for the door. As I swung my legs out into the parking lot, I felt a cool draft blowing in the front of my pants. Glancing down to find out why, I was shocked to find that the zipper of my pants had broken, thus leaving me exposed for the entire world to see.

Suddenly I had a sick feeling in my stomach. It was imperative that I be there to represent the department. If I wasn't, the cases scheduled for that day could be dismissed. I began to panic. There wasn't time enough to beat feet back to Burnham for a quick change of britches; what the hell was I going to do?

Slipping into the office, I was cordially greeted by Donna, the clerk of courts who handled all of the legal affairs for the courthouse. I had only recently met Donna for the first time, and I really didn't know her from Adam, but from my first impression, she appeared to be a fun-loving, hell-raising individual who didn't give two hoots about much of anything. She was loud, loved to joke around, and was definitely full of the devil.

Entering her office, I was quite relieved to see that she was the only one there at this early hour . . . for the time being, anyway. I was walking like a wounded duck with my hands placed securely over the fly of my pants and my summons book covering my front end. I quickly introduced myself to her once again, advising her that I was the court officer for the Fish and Game Department for that morning. Then, red-faced, I humbly stated that I had a serious problem.

"What's the matter, honey?" she politely inquired.

I quickly explained the problem with my zipper, and the fact that I didn't have enough time to return to Burnham for another change of clothes. I couldn't possibly stand in front of the courtroom filled with all of those people with my fly wide open. I was in a quandary.

"What the hell am I going to do?" I asked.

Smirking, Donna barked, "Oh, for cripe's sake, go into the closet over there, take your pants off, and pass them out to me. I'll fix 'em for you!"

Now, I have to tell you—for a rookie warden just starting what would hopefully be a long and rewarding career, doing exactly as she asked was quite an undertaking . . . especially with a lady I'd just met. But then again, what other choice did I have? She seemed genuinely willing to help.

I shot into the closet where the officers normally hung their coats when they came to the courthouse. Quickly I removed my pants and handed them out through a small crack in the door. Modesty was of the greatest concern to me; it always had been. I was petrified someone would find me standing in the clerk of courts closet with no pants on. Never in the blue hinges of hell would I be able to talk my way out of it—no more than I'd have been willing to believe anyone else in a similar circumstance had the shoe been on the other foot.

Snatching the trousers out of my hand, Donna said, "There you go, honey—that's the last time you'll see those babies!"

I hoped she was kidding. (It sounded like she was, but how would I know?) I wrapped my heavy red wool coat around my half-naked body, just in case someone—like the judge—opened the door. I shuddered at the thought. The anxiety of standing half-naked in the courtroom closet waiting for my pants to be repaired was almost more than I could bear (no pun intended).

I managed to keep one ear pushed up against the door, trying to hear if anyone was approaching. At the same time, I was silently rehearsing what I'd say if someone found me standing there without pants.

Suddenly I heard male voices coming into the office. I recognized them as a couple of state trooper buddies whom I'd recently met, but barely knew. Harry Bailey was one of them. What little I knew about Harry, I knew damn well that if he found me standing there without pants, he'd automatically think I was involved in something kinky going on at the courthouse. And why wouldn't he?

Then I heard Trooper Bob Bragg enter the office. He began harassing Harry about some foolish thing they had done the previous day. Neither one of them had a clue as to the mystery unfolding in the little closet adjacent to where they were now standing. I expected the door to fly open at any minute, and there I'd be! The sweat was running down my forehead and my scrawny legs were shaking like a bowl of Jell-O as I wrapped the coat a little tighter around my body.

After what seemed like an eternity, Donna finally came waltzing out of her office with my pants firmly clutched in her hands. "Your britches are all done, John," she hollered as she pounded on the closed closet door. "If you want 'em, come out here and get 'em; they're on my desk!" She snickered deviously. There was an eerie silence that fell upon the clerk's office, as I'm sure by this point Harry and Bob were trying to figure out what the hell was going on here.

I quickly opened the door, ready to make a mad dash to her desk and back, only to have

Donna pass my pants directly to me. Remarkably, the fly was fixed and my day was saved. Dressing as quickly as I could, I emerged from the closet only to be greeted by a host of wise-arse comments and smirks from my partners in uniform.

I really don't know if Harry and Bob believed the story as it had happened or not. At least they were the only ones to have witnessed the event. With this latest crisis behind me I could now be the court officer without fear of being held in contempt by the judge . . . contempt for, of all things, indecent exposure.

The Rubber Hand

Eventually I became quite complacent about my duties at the courthouse, including how to deal with those who managed and scheduled judicial events.

Judge Edwin Smith from Bar Harbor was the magistrate assigned to the Belfast District Court. "Smitty," as we called him, presided in court every Tuesday and Friday. He may have been amicable away from the bench, but in the court-room he was a stern old bugger who demanded professionalism and order. In most cases he kept to himself and was strictly business.

One morning just before Halloween, and before Smitty arrived in his chambers, Maine state trooper Harry Bailey and I were waiting for arraignments to begin. Harry had confiscated an old rubber hand from someone, part of a Halloween costume that looked quite real. The rubber glove was covered with warts, cuts, and blisters, and looked like it had been chopped off the arm of some monster character out of a horror movie. The hand was as realistic-looking as anything I'd ever seen before, and we found ourselves raising hell with it in the clerk's office while waiting for the day's activities to commence.

Someone suggested we sneak into the judge's private chambers and jam the horrid-looking hand in his bathroom door. Thinking it might give the judge a laugh to start his day, I volunteered to be the one to commit the dastardly deed. Harry played lookout in the hallway as I shot into the judge's chambers, quickly opened his bathroom door, and slammed the grotesque-looking hand between the door and the doorjamb. Chuckling to myself like a kid who had just pulled the prank of the century upon an unsuspecting friend, I scurried out of the room and back into the clerk's office, quite proud of what I had just done.

A few minutes later, Smitty shuffled down the hallway and into his chambers. Within seconds, the telephone intercom between Donna's office and the judge was buzzing. Donna answered with the customary, "Good morning, Your

Honor!" It was rather obvious from the expression on her face that the conversation wasn't going well.

"Yes, Your Honor, I'll pass the message along, Your Honor! We will see that it is taken care of immediately, sir. Yes sir, I will." And with that she terminated the call.

Rather disgustedly she stared at Harry and me as she yelled, "I don't know which one of you damn clowns put that rubber hand in the judge's bathroom door, but you'd better go in there and take it out—right now! He's not any too happy!"

Uh-oh! This wasn't good. I looked at Harry and said, "It's your damn hand, and it was you who talked me into doing it. Now it's your turn to go in and get it."

"Bullshit," he said, smirking. I'd seen that grin before whenever he thought someone was about to get into trouble. "No way am I going in there! I didn't put the damn thing in there, and I'm not about to take it out and get the blame."

With that, I knew I had to be the one to make a move. Slowly, I hiked across the hall and opened the door to the judge's chambers. He was sitting at his desk intently watching my every move. He kind of reminded me of a damned mean old cat about ready to pounce on a poor, helpless mouse. Hoping to break the ice, I cheerfully said "Good morning, Your Honor" as I walked briskly past his desk and over to the bathroom door, quickly grabbing ahold of the rubber hand and pulling it away from the doorjamb. I wanted to say, "Harry asked me to come and get this for him," but I thought better of it.

Smitty never said a word, but he glared at me over the top of his glasses. I could feel the hair standing up on the back of my neck and felt like a mouse about to be pounced on at any minute. With the rubber hand in tow I quickly backed out of his office, seeking safe refuge in the clerk's office.

"What did he say? What did he say?" Harry asked.

Disgusted, I responded, "Nothing, Harry—absolutely nothing! I think I'm in deep shit." And I was. It was several weeks before Smitty went my way on a questionable legal ruling.

In reality, Judge Smith was an outstanding professional, extremely fair, honest, and firm. He ran his courtroom the way it should be run. Even though his sense of humor may have been lacking a little, I had developed the utmost respect for the man, and truly found him to be an exceptional person. Whenever one of us got out of line, we had no one to blame but ourselves. I certainly deserved my time of being blackballed by the magistrate.

I have to *hand* it to him (no pun intended)—he certainly got his point across without ever uttering a word.

The Echoing "Thunder Clap"

Have you ever experienced one of those moments when something truly hilarious occurs and you lose total control over your emotions, such as laughing out loud when you are expected to refrain and be quiet? This was the case at the district court one Tuesday morning just as the court's business was beginning to be heard.

The small courtroom was packed with a variety of folks who were waiting for their moment to stand before Smitty and enter their pleas to the charges pending against them. There was such a crowd that a few of us officers were required to lean up against the wall as we waited our turn to testify. Smitty, who wore hearing aids, sometimes didn't hear everything that was going on around him, especially when the courtroom was crowded and noisy. He showed his frustration by suddenly banging his wooden gavel on the bench, demanding order in his courtroom.

On this particular day there was a rather large and somewhat obese lady seated in the very front row of the courtroom. She was all by herself, seeing as she nearly filled the entire hard wooden bench she was perched upon. Smitty had just begun calling the docket, and one by one, the defendants stood before him, entering their pleas. Due to the large crowd seated inside the courtroom I was forced to lean up against the wall by the swinging doors that led out into the hallway.

Over on the other side of the room, Searsport police chief Al Leavitt was also leaning up against the wall, watching events as they happened. Court officer Roy Thomas was standing near the judge's bench, shuffling through the papers that were being handed to him by the judge. I happened to glance over toward the obese lady seated on the hard wooden bench not far from where I was standing just as she leaned to her right and then back to her left. As she did this, she discharged a blast of gas that created a sound similar to a small clap of thunder. In simple layman's terms, she had farted.

The unexpected noise echoed throughout the courtroom. The woman never batted an eye as she nonchalantly kept staring straight ahead, as if nothing had happened. Those folks seated nearby began snickering among themselves. Within seconds, nearly everyone inside the courtroom was laughing uncontrollably, myself included. It was definitely one of those hysterical moments when a person loses all self-control, no matter how hard he tries to maintain some semblance of dignity.

The laughter got louder and louder once everyone realized what had caused the clap of thunder to echo throughout the small courtroom. I immediately escaped through the swinging doors and into the hallway, trying as best I could to contain my own hysteria.

The judge, who apparently didn't know what had caused this sudden burst of laughter inside his courtroom, was sternly glaring over the top of his glasses at the mass of folks seated before him, trying to figure out why everyone was laughing. He demanded order in his courtroom as he loudly pounded his gavel in disgust.

Poor Al Leavitt was desperately attempting to work his way across the courtroom, heading toward the exit where I had gone. He was obviously trying to maintain his composure as he quickly scurried across the aisle.

I stood outside the door, still laughing uncontrollably. Peeking through the windows back into the courtroom, my eyes made direct contact with Al's as he hastily scrambled toward the exit. That was all it took; he lost complete control, laughing out loud along with the others still seated inside. By now we were both guffawing so hard that tears were streaming down our cheeks. He burst through the door just in time to hear poor Roy Thomas desperately trying to get folks to calm down.

By now, Roy himself was on the verge of losing control—not so much because of what this lady had done to cause such a disturbance, but more because of the comedic nature of the situation itself, with everybody laughing so uproariously.

Judge Smith was still totally oblivious as to what had happened. Hastily, he called an immediate recess as he returned to his chambers in disgust. By now Roy had joined us in the hallway, and we were all gasping for breath. We found ourselves laughing at each other rather than what had transpired inside the courtroom.

As for the lady whose shot of "laughing gas" brought about a quick ending to the normal routine of the Belfast District Court, through it all she remained planted in the front row, staring straight ahead and acting as if nothing had happened.

The Rolling Parachute

I'm sure that some of you folks who've had military careers at one time or another may have been subjected to live ammunition fire. Whether the experience occurred during training or actual combat, I'd be willing to bet that you still remember it well.

On a November evening in 1980, I experienced a similar situation while working night-hunters in the Burnham area, which had been experiencing a fair amount of night activity recently. I was parked in a large field, and my partner, Norman Gilbert, was working in a separate field close by. We had decided to work separate locations for the evening, figuring it might enhance our chances of catching those involved. On this particular night, the department aircraft was also flying high overhead throughout the division, hoping to further assist us in our efforts.

I was neatly snuggled in behind a small island of brush located in the center of the large field near the Unity/Burnham town line. It was the perfect place to park, being fairly close to the highway where I could quickly catch up to an offending vehicle if they did happen to commit the dirty deed.

It was a clear and extremely cold night as I sat alone in my cruiser, watching the bright stars twinkling high up overhead. I could hear a howling pack of coyotes off in the woods behind me as well as an occasional hoot from an owl perched nearby. All in all, it was what I considered to be a relaxing time spent underneath the heavens.

In order to prevent the chrome on my cruiser from giving away my location should a beam of light be cast out into the field, I had covered the front end of the car with a cut-up nylon parachute. The drab-colored chute was ideal in accomplishing this task. As I sat in the cruiser listening to the radio traffic throughout the state, I was thoroughly enjoying the peace and tranquility of the night. Nothing was more satisfying than kicking back and relaxing without the interference of a telephone or the other distractions of normal everyday living.

It was nearly one o'clock in the morning when I heard what sounded like a muffled rifle shot fairly close by. Soon afterward, a vehicle slowly approached the area at a crawl. Suddenly a large beam of light was cast out from the window, illuminating the field and scanning back and forth alongside the cruiser and the field around me. *Night-hunters for sure,* I thought. I quickly awoke from the pleasant dreamland I'd been in, wondering what would happen next.

As the beam of the light slowly reached my location, a sudden gust of wind caused the parachute to blow outward and flop away from the front end of my cruiser. Suddenly I heard three loud snaps, followed by *ka-pow! ka-pow! ka-pow!* I could hear the bullets zinging past the open window of my cruiser as I quickly dove behind the dashboard, hoping the shots wouldn't penetrate the windshield. My heart was pounding like never before as I reached for the police radio to advise Norman that I was being shot at. I directed him to set up a roadblock at a certain point up ahead on the highway, where I knew the hunters would be heading.

The crew's vehicle slowly proceeded along on the highway, illuminating the field below me. Obviously they were satisfied they hadn't struck the moving object illuminated by their bright light. I quickly exited the cruiser, ripping the nylon parachute off my car and tossing it down on the ground. Immediately I shot out of that field without lights and onto the highway, attempting to catch up with these perpetrators as they slowly cruised along in front of me. Using their taillights as a guide, in no time at all I was directly behind them.

By now, they were illuminating another series of fields, completely oblivious to the fact that I was cruising along only a few feet behind them, glued to their back bumper like a wart on a toad's rump. Initiating the blue lights, siren, and head-lights on my cruiser all at the same time, the quiet Burnham night suddenly erupted into a high-speed chase.

Norman was already close to his destination as I told him I was pursuing the offenders. By now we were traveling at speeds of over ninety miles per hour on the narrow country road, headed directly toward the roadblock Norman was establishing a short distance away.

Off in the distance the flashing blue lights of Norman's cruiser suddenly appeared. He had blocked the road as best he could with his parked car, in order to prevent them from having an escape route. Just the sight of his cruiser was a welcome sight, knowing that someone from my side was waiting nearby.

As we approached the roadblock the offending vehicle suddenly skidded to an abrupt stop a short distance away from Norman's cruiser. One of the men jumped out of the car toting a rifle and took off running into the woods just as fast as his little legs would carry him. The vehicle then drove on up to Norman's cruiser, pulling over to the side of the road as if nothing was wrong.

I had heard from state trooper Dennis Hayden on the radio, so I knew that he and his canine Skipper, who were patrolling nearby, were on their way. They would help us capture the missing bandito who had run into the woods.

In the meantime, Norman and I placed the two remaining occupants from inside the vehicle in handcuffs and led them to the confinement of our cruisers. They were both extremely intoxicated, and, as was typical of some of these offenders, they adamantly denied having any other accomplices, and of course, "There was no freaking way they'd been night-hunting."

"How to hell you gonna prove that bullshit, when you don't even have any solid evidence? You know, something like maybe a gun, or ammunition?" one of the men boldly inquired. It was obvious they'd been down this route before, and knew there would be no case without the proper evidence to convict them.

The adrenaline rush I'd experienced as the bullets flew past my window had somewhat subsided by now. Rather than contaminating the area by rushing off to pursue the escapee, we wisely decided to await the arrival of Dennis and his dog, Skipper, before beginning a foot chase into the woods. One thing was certain: Without a light, the fleeing offender wouldn't get very far. This particular section of woods was extremely wet and thick, and the entire area was covered with alders and dense brush.

We quickly determined that our two detainees were well-noted criminals from the surrounding area. They had served time for a bank robbery they'd committed in the rural community of

Hartland a few years earlier. As convicted felons, by law neither of them were allowed to be in possession of a firearm.

With the arrival of Trooper Hayden and Skipper, I made a solemn pledge: "Dennis, old boy, if you and Skipper get this guy, I'll buy you a case of any kind of beer you want!"

"You've got a deal!" Dennis shouted, as he quickly prepared Skipper to perform his duties. Advising me to stay well behind them, together we trudged off into the thick woods, following the path taken by the fugitive. Norman stayed back at the vehicles, guarding the other two detainees.

Within a few minutes, Dennis turned around with a big grin on his face. "John Boy, I'll take a case of Heineken!" he shouted, as he forcefully snagged the third suspect out from behind the old rotten log he was hiding behind. Lying beside him was the loaded rifle that would help to cinch the charges levied against these men.

This crew of three night-hunters became the newest notch carved into the base of my metal flashlight, denoting those captured in the act of doing a little night-hunting. With each outfit I picked up, I made it a custom to grind a notch in the metal flashlight, similar to what many old-time fighter pilots did during wartime after they had successfully shot down an enemy aircraft.

The Secret

During the late evening hours of November 11th, 1976, while working with Warden Lowell Thomas, we managed to capture three non-resident folks in the act of night hunting just outside the town of Unity.

These Connecticut residents were caught red-handed in a compromising situation of illuminating fields with a hand held spotlight, while possessing a loaded rifle beside them.

I was quite familiar with them as being cronies of my friend Harold, who had a camp at Unity Pond. Every fall this same group of hunters came to the area.

These men were actually members of the same hunting camp gang that brought about the title for my first book, *Suddenly the Cider Didn't Taste So Good*, as they made the Academy Award presentation of returning my wardens cap and explaining where the apples came from, for the cider I was drinking.

I had a gut feeling that any one of these hunters could possibly be future candidates for violating the laws I was asked to enforce.

We had an understanding between us—that should they step over the line, I'd show no partiality in performing my duties—a fact which they accepted without a lot of negative commentary.

A little before midnight on that November night, three of them did cross that line as they searched for a deer under the beam of a bright spotlight.

While Lowell and I attended to the legal actions against these men, we received a rather cool reception. They knew they were in a heap of trouble as they forfeited their firearm to the state of Maine, along with $500 each and a sentence to spend three days in the county slammer.

The next morning all three appeared at the Belfast District Court, where they entered guilty pleas to the charges. They humbly begged the court for a deferral of time before they'd have to serve their jail sentences. I spoke to the judge on their behalf, asking for the sentence to be deferred to a weekend selected by the court to accommodate these men with regards to their employment.

The judge agreed, advising the three to report to the Waldo County Jail on a Friday evening in February of 1977, to complete the rest of their obligation to the state of Maine.

"If you fail to show," the judge emphasized, "an arrest warrant will be issued for each of you, and you will be taken to a facility where your incarceration might be increased," he sternly warned the three of them.

They assured the magistrate they'd arrive on the date he'd selected.

We shook hands in the hallway afterwards, as they apologized, with assurances they'd learned a valuable lesson. I had no doubt but what they had, although I was never invited back to the camp for another home-cooked meal.

Months passed, when at 1 a.m. one Saturday morning in late February, I received a phone call from the Maine State Police headquarters in Augusta.

"Warden Ford, we have an attempt to locate a party of three men who are supposedly staying at a camp on the shores of Unity Pond, in Unity. According to their wives, their husbands are staying there for the purpose of making repairs to their hunting camp.

"These women have repeatedly tried to contact their husbands, but have been unable to. They haven't heard a word from them since they left Connecticut, and now they're afraid that something drastic has happened to their loved ones. Could you possibly go to the area to do a welfare check on them?" the dispatcher inquired.

Groggily I said, "Okay, I'll get dressed and be right out. You can give me the directions on how to get to the area when I sign on the radio," I disgustedly grumbled.

It was bitterly cold outside. The last thing I wanted to do was to head out into the back-country to try to find someone, but the thought entered my mind that maybe carbon monoxide poisoning or some other tragic event might have overcome these men.

I quickly donned my uniform, heading to my cruiser for the journey northward. As I climbed inside, I requested the information of where to go and who I was looking for from the State Police dispatcher. By then, I was wide awake and better prepared to understand exactly where I was going.

Once I was given directions, I quickly headed that way. As I drove along, I inquired as to who I'd be looking for. "You'll be looking for Nelson, Stephen, and John . . ." Before they could give me the last names, a little light came on in my head. These three men weren't going to be found at a camp in Unity but rather serving their sentences behind bars at the Waldo County Jail.

Apparently, they'd never disclosed the real reason to their wives back home as to why they were coming north. Instead, they made up an excuse—the camp was in dire need of repairs, and this was the weekend they'd chosen to make those repairs. In reality, they were fulfilling their obligation to the State of Maine for their illegal actions of the previous fall.

I quickly checked with the county jail to make

sure they were all snuggled in a cell before advising the State Police of my conclusion. And they were!

I was asked to call the alarmed wives in Connecticut to explain the situation to them, relieving their fears.

Needless to say, my nonresident hunting buddies' little secret was exposed. There was a trio of extremely angry and scared women back in Connecticut, ready to seek justice of their own.

The next morning, I felt an obligation to meet with the three men at the jail just to inform them of this latest turn of events. Without a doubt, these guys dreaded the return back home a lot more than the jail sentence that had been given to them by the judge in Maine.

Something told me their problems were just beginning.

From that day forward, I suspected my welcome at the hunting camp would never be what it once was.

Adding insult to injury, one of the wives forwarded to yours truly a copy of the fake newspaper they had made with a huge headline that read NELSON, STEVE, AND JOHN, CONVICTED OF NIGHT-HUNTING IN MAINE, SENTENCED TO WALDO COUNTY JAIL.

Several copies of this fake newspaper with its bold headline had been posted at locations where these three men often congregated, including the fish and game club where they were members and the local bar that they frequently patronized. All of their friends had been made aware of their run-in with the wardens in Maine, thanks to the devious actions of some very distraught and now very vindictive wives.

The moral of the story is quite simple: It's not nice trying to hold little secrets from your wives —you'll pay big-time in the end.

If you don't believe it, I know three out-of-state hunters who will undoubtedly verify this fact.

Caught in a Lie

As a new recruit, during the early days of my profession I was still in a so-called probationary period for a designated amount of time, usually one year. During this time my activities were closely monitored and evaluated by my boss, George Nash, to see whether I was conforming to the department's standards. One of my winter duties was performing a weekly check of known deer yards in my district—something I usually did alone, although on occasion, George would join me.

The purpose of checking the deer yards was to ensure that the deer herd was healthy and not being harassed by house dogs, bobcats, or other predators. For those of you wondering what a deer yard is, it's a place where cedar and the normal feed for deer are abundant and readily available for their needs. These yards are situated in an area where the deer can bed down and travel back and forth along well-packed trails in the deep snow, making it less stressful for them during the long, cold winter months, a time when they find themselves most vulnerable to the cruel acts of Mother Nature.

Coyotes had not yet infiltrated the region in the early 1970s, so the problems associated with the harassment of deer were not as common-place in those days as what they've since become. Bobcats and the common house dog proved to be the most aggressive critters to invade a deer yard, raising havoc upon the herd.

We wardens depended upon our State-issued snowshoes to perform this weekly task as we trudged through the deep snow, counting and logging in on our daily reports the numbers of rabbits, deer, grouse, or other species of game we happened to encounter on our travels. I truly enjoyed a casual jaunt into the woods, observing and counting the wildlife around me, but to have to do it on a weekly basis was getting to be a real pain in the you-know-what.

I voiced my concern to my fellow warden, Bill, who had far more experience than I. He laughed and said, "Hell, John, don't be forcing yourself to go out into the woods every week; no one else does. Just log in your daily reports that you've made your checks and then take an educated guess as to how many deer or other species of game you would have seen. That's what the rest of us do. They'll never know the difference in Augusta, and besides, we have too damn many chores to maintain as it is without making this one a priority."

His advice sounded good to me. If all the other wardens were doing this, why shouldn't I? I certainly was finding plenty of other things to occupy my time without spending the better part of a day walking around the same old trails.

One of the largest deer yards in my district was located in an area known as the Leonard Woods, situated between Waterville Road along Unity Plantation and Winnecook Road in Burnham, covering some six to eight miles of thick woods. On a typical day I'd see a hundred deer or more as they traveled along their packed trails in the deep snow, or along the skidder trails created by woodcutters harvesting in the area. It certainly was a sight to behold!

One cold January morning my supervisor, George Nash, decided to join me for a hike out into this large deer yard. By day's end George was totally amazed at the large number of deer we had seen wandering all around us. Even though we were completely exhausted upon returning to his vehicle, it had been a most enjoyable day for both of us. I had the privilege of spending some quality time with my new boss, getting to know him better, and he in turn got to know me. At day's end we parted company on great terms as George dropped me off at the warden's camp and he headed back to Old Town, where he lived.

For the next few weeks I followed my neighboring warden's advice, fudging my reports in regard to checking the deer yards. I boldly logged numbers into my daily reports, indicating that I'd walked X amount of miles on my snowshoes and had seen X amount of deer and other game during my travels. I based my figures on what George and I had experienced a few weeks before, while in reality, I never went near the area. What the hell? If the rest of my cronies were doing it, I guess I could. Like Bill said, "They'll never know the difference in Augusta!"

Some four or five weeks after Supervisor Nash and I had spent the day together in the Leonard Woods, observing scores of deer cautiously parading around us, he arrived back at the camp early one morning. George was quite jovial as he jokingly inquired if I'd just crawled out of bed, and whether I had the coffeepot on.

"I'm doing an employee evaluation today, and there are a few issues I have to discuss with you," he said calmly. Sitting at the kitchen table a few minutes later, coffee cup in hand, he said, "John, I want to commend you for the great job you're doing thus far. In the little time you've been with the department, you've made great strides in your public relations, and certainly in the caliber of your work."

To receive such complimentary words of encouragement from the boss was quite an honor, and, more than that, a relief. I hoped this meant I'd soon complete my probationary period and finally become a permanent member of the agency I loved so much. God almighty, my head was swelling with pride as my boss laid all of this high praise and glory upon me. I was quite pleased that he felt this way, as it would be his decision as to whether I'd make it through the probationary period or not.

"Now, John, I'm really impressed with your deer-yard checks. This task is quite vital to managing the herd and making sure they are all doing well during the long winter months."

I smiled even as I squirmed a bit, knowing how I'd fudged the numbers.

After a brief pause, George asked matter-of-factly, "Oh, by the way, John—how many pair of snowshoes do you currently have?"

"I just have the one pair the department issued me," I stated, wondering why he would even ask such a question.

"Oh, really? Just the one pair?"

I nodded. "Why do you ask?" I said.

Smiling like a fox about ready to pounce on its prey, George said, "Well, as I said, we've been impressed with your deer-yard reports over the past few weeks; you've really been doing a tremendous job, just as we expect you to. But I was kind of wondering how you've been doing it, seeing as the last time we were together, you forgot your snowshoes in the trunk of my car. That's where they've been until today . . . so I thought I'd bring them back to you." He smirked, and his eyes had that devious "Gotcha!" look.

Great gobs of guppy poop, I'd been caught in my own trap! I could hear Bill's voice echoing in my ears: "Just fudge your reports like the rest of us; they'll never know in Augusta." So much for seeking advice from a neighboring partner in crime . . . but then again, how could I blame him for my own stupidity? I found myself trying to swallow my hot coffee as if it were laced with arsenic.

I could tell George was proud to have proven his point, although he didn't let me suffer long before telling me that my job was secure; better yet, my probationary period had ended. Before leaving, he chuckled warmly and confided that under the same circumstances many years ago, prior to becoming a supervisor, he'd done the same thing with his reports. He didn't encourage me to continue walking down the path of deceit, and stressed the fact that he hoped I'd learned a valuable lesson.

I assured him that I had. *If nothing else,* I thought to myself, *I'll be damn smart enough the next time around to make sure I always have my snowshoes in my possession!*

Something Fishy Here

It was unusually hot one late spring, and on one of my few trips out to Unity Pond that season, checking fishermen and boaters for licenses and safety equipment, I'd left my vehicle parked at the public boat landing at the lake. The white perch were in the middle of their annual spawn, and as a result of this activity, they were biting quite well.

The abundance of so many perch gathering along the shoreline allowed fishermen to gather great buckets full of these fish. Seeing as where there was no limit on white perch, many folks and their siblings were having a grand old time, enjoying their sport. Some folks planned on making a good homemade fish chowder from their day's efforts, while others would use their catch as fertilizer for their gardens. All of them were having fun, pulling in one perch after another.

As my cruiser sat unprotected in the parking lot, I slowly made my way around the shore of the pond, chatting with folks along the way. All in all, it was a rather enjoyable day. Eventually I made my way back to the boat landing and my cruiser, heading for the comforts of home.

A few days later I began to notice a putrid smell coming from somewhere inside my car, but I couldn't seem to locate the cause. I noticed that every time I drove the vehicle it seemed to be getting a little worse. I spent hours washing and vacuuming the inside of the cruiser, including the trunk, where I'd occasionally place a decaying dead deer or another wild critter's carcass to be carted off to a different location. But even after all the washings, the moment I drove the cruiser, the smell returned.

As spring turned to summer, the smell continued to get much worse, to the point where I actually dreaded driving the cruiser. I just couldn't seem to find the source of the stench. I was purchasing air fresheners by the gross, in addition to trying every type of cleaning fluid I could get my hands on, but nothing was working.

Finally, late one afternoon as I was patrolling an old back road, I had the misfortune of having a flat tire. Pulling the cruiser over to the side of the narrow dirt road, I found myself somewhat relieved to be standing outside in the fresh air, changing a tire, away from that sickening smell.

Much to my surprise, as I popped off the hubcap to my tire I located the cause of my odor problem. Encased within the hubcap and the wheel was a thick, putrid-smelling goo, stuck to the insides. The hubcaps were filled with fish—white perch, to be exact. By the hubcaps, I mean all four. Someone had filled them with fish and had set me up real good! No wonder the stench only got worse whenever I started to drive. The more I drove, the worse it got.

I quickly removed the fishy mess and gave the wheels a thorough washing. Finally I had my cruiser back to the point where I could once again cruise the area without wanting to vomit.

I knew if I remained silent long enough, someone in the community wouldn't be able to stand it and would have to ask whether or not I'd found the fish. Besides, I didn't want to give anyone the sheer satisfaction of knowing just how uncomfortable I'd really been these past few weeks.

The silence paid off when a young fellow working at a local garage brought up the subject of my fishy hubcaps one day as I was filling my vehicle with fuel. My eyes widened. I was onto something here! How did he come to know about this little prank, and furthermore, just how much did he really know? With a little luck, I might be able to solve this fishy mystery once and for all.

To make a long story short, I coerced him into taking a short ride in my cruiser, which at the time he was glad to accept. It wasn't quite a kidnapping, but it was some damn close! We drove to a remote area on a dead-end road, to a place far away from any witnesses or folks that might overhear our conversation. We then proceeded to have a nice little conversation just between us, one where I was doing most of the talking and he was doing some serious listening.

Within a few minutes he'd 'fessed up to being one of the two culprits who had so cleverly devised this little prank—a case where they had decided to have a little fun with their new local game warden. This was yet another one of those prime examples of confession being good for the soul, as I detected a great sense of relief from the expression on his face, once he'd admitted his sin.

We departed the remote woods road that day with an agreement between us: He'd contact his buddy and, depending upon their willingness to cooperate fully, we would meet at a place of their convenience to discuss just how this matter would best be resolved. I figured it would be a punishment far removed from the judicial system, which I'm sure they feared now that their little prank had been exposed.

The meeting occurred as planned. The guilty parties begged for leniency, and in the end, the new local game warden made two new friends. (In the process I also managed to get my cruiser washed for nothing whenever I deemed it necessary.)

In all honesty, I privately admired the courage

of these young men for undertaking such a bold move in the first place. It was indeed a good, harmless prank, one that caused annoyance more than anything else. God bless our youth and their ingenuity. Had I been in their shoes I doubt I'd have been smart enough to come up with such a gimmick.

Mike and Terry were not known for being wild or displaying a total disrespect for the laws and the lawmen enforcing them, as were some folks in the community. They were just a couple of congenial country boys who enjoyed life in the fast lane as they tried to decide just where their futures would take them.

As a result of this little encounter, we developed a mutual friendship between us that continued for years. There were even a few occasions where they went out on patrol with their local warden.

Sadly, a few years later Mike was killed in a car crash outside of Unity. I was one of the first responders to arrive at the horrible scene. I departed the area that night feeling as if I'd lost a good friend, and in essence, I had.

Harvesting the Weed

After twelve years as a warden, changes regarding the duties we performed as law enforcement officers were occurring quite frequently. During this time there was a sudden explosion of self-taught horticulturists dabbling in the art of illegally growing marijuana plants in our woods. The marijuana market was thriving, and these folks were taking advantage of it, challenging society's rules and trying to make a quick buck. There was no lack of customers, that's for sure.

In previous months, plants had sprung up in overgrown fields, along small country streams, and in many remote woodlots. Large patches of marijuana were popping up seemingly out of nowhere. Some of these crops appeared destined for the gardeners' personal use. However, due to the size of some of these plots, it was obvious the gardeners intended to sell their product to those who smoked the illicit material and didn't want to risk raising their own crop.

Late one August afternoon in 1983, a local hunter stopped by my residence. He said he'd accidentally wandered into a large patch of "funny-looking plants" stashed out behind a young man's rented home in the town of Jackson.

"I ain't never seen plants like that before. I think it's that damned stuff they call marijuana," he said excitedly. "The stuff I wandered into ain't nothing that's growing wild or naturally. Every plant is about head-high. They look like full-bloomed Christmas trees, all staked up and surrounded by chicken wire. Some of them have tags on them with a variety of funny-looking names. I made sure I got to hell out of there some quick."

Being vaguely familiar with the location, I knew the young man residing on the property was known to occasionally indulge in a smoke or two of his own. In the past he had been convicted of trafficking in the illegal material.

The next day, accompanied by Scott Sienkiewicz, my trusted deputy warden, I conducted a search of the area in question. It wasn't long before we stumbled across the large patch of greenery my friend had described. It was like nothing I'd ever seen before: There were between thirty and forty plants, all of them well-groomed and staked, just as he'd described. I broke off a large sample from one of the plants, verifying what we'd found.

Contacting a Maine State Police buddy, Mark Nickerson, I advised him as to how this wasn't a normal find of a few homegrown plants for someone's personal use. These plants were well-manicured, sticky to the touch, and heavily loaded with buds. By far, they were some of the best-quality plants we'd ever seen. I suspected the culprit responsible to be the young man renting the small house adjacent to the patch of woods.

"How can we catch him tending the plants in order to prove they're his?" Mark inquired.

Utilizing a little cop ingenuity, we came up with a plan to hopefully draw our suspect directly to his crop. It needed to be well executed, leaving no doubt as to whose pot it was. The plan was as follows: The very next day, Scott and I would sneak back into the area into a place where we could observe the marijuana patch. Mark, accompanied by Sergeant Gary Boynton of the Waldo County sheriff's office, would remain nearby, out of sight and in their cruisers, for communication and assistance. They would be ready to assist whenever we gave them the word. Once in place, we'd advise them we were ready to carry out our mission. Mark would go to my house, placing an anonymous phone call to the store in Brooks, where our suspect worked.

Mark would simply say, "Hey, you don't know me, but I have a little word of advice for you. I was down at the courthouse earlier today and overheard the cops trying to get a search warrant for the marijuana plants growing out behind your house. You might want to get there before they do." Then he'd hang up, hoping this was enough to entice our suspect into taking the bait.

As luck would have it, Warden Pilot Dana Toothaker was overhead in the department aircraft. We solicited his expertise in becoming our eyes in the sky to observe the store where our suspect was working. He could advise us if the suspect had taken the bait and was en route to protect his stash.

Within minutes of implementing the plan, we heard from Mark. "The call's been made."

Dana was circling high up over Brooks. Sergeant Boynton was monitoring the radio traffic nearby, waiting to spring into action. Scott and I were nestled a few feet apart, hiding underneath the low-hanging branches of a couple of large hemlock trees, situated in the middle of the marijuana patch. It was show-and-tell time.

Suddenly the radio came to life. "Your suspect just ran out of the store," said Dana. "He's jumped into his van and is quickly coming your way."

My heart was pounding in anticipation.

Dana followed the suspect from high overhead, reporting all along the way: "He's pulling into the dooryard. Now he's armed with a chain saw, and he's felling trees directly across the field road beside his house. It appears he's trying to prevent traffic from entering the old overgrown field near where you guys are located. I'm going to back out of here for now, so as not to spook him," Dana said.

We could hear the chain saw revving as trees started toppling a short distance away. Dana's role in the mission, a vital and informative one, was completed, but as soon as he'd departed the area, none of us had any idea what was occurring.

By now the chain saw had fallen quiet. A few minutes later, I thought I heard a noise a short distance away, almost as if someone was climbing a tree, but from where we were concealed, I couldn't be sure. There was a hunter's tree stand a short distance away, located along the edge of the overgrown field.

For the next ninety minutes, there was nothing but dead silence. I knew my trooper buddy Mark would be getting impatient, but I advised him to stay put. I felt that someone was lurking nearby, but I couldn't tell for sure. Mark had the patience of a dog in heat when it came to waiting for something to happen, and I knew I had to convince him to give it a little more time, which surprisingly I was able to accomplish.

Suddenly, there were footsteps quietly coming our way. I was lying underneath a hemlock tree near a marijuana plant—the same one I'd ripped a branch from, to use for identification purposes. Seemingly out of nowhere I saw the legs and boots of a man standing at the plant, just a few feet away. He was muttering to himself. "What the hell . . . ?" as he noticed the missing limb. It was time to spring into action. I quickly slid out from underneath the hemlock tree and advised him, "Game warden—hold it right there! You're under arrest."

I found myself face-to-face with an angry man holding a large machete in one hand, heading my way. He was obviously a bit startled by the intrusion into his private garden. As he continued walking toward me, ignoring my orders to stand to, Scott emerged from his position, jacking a live round into the twelve-gauge shotgun he was toting.

We quickly subdued and searched the intruder, surprised to find a loaded nine-millimeter pistol tucked inside the waist of his pants. Once he was handcuffed and we were in control of the situation, I advised Mark and Gary that the mission was accomplished. It was time for them to join us.

Accidentally stumbling onto one of these areas always presented a certain amount of danger to those invading the grow operation. Some of these cleverly placed plots were booby-trapped with hazards that could severely injure trespassers. In this case, our patience paid off. The three agencies working together proved how effective coordinated teamwork can be. (I was totally amazed that I was able to convince my buddy Mark to stay in one spot for a couple of hours— a major feat in itself!)

Sergeant Boynton hauled the man off to the

county jail and we began cutting and documenting the illegal crop. The load of marijuana was transported to Augusta for testing and to be documented as evidence. The estimated value of these plants was several thousand dollars. At that time, they were by far the best-manicured and most potent plants ever recovered in these parts in an outdoor-grow operation.

The Snowmobile
and the Hood

I shared a secret once with a few of my so-called "real" friends, regarding one of my early snow-mobiling adventures. These friends said I'd never be able to share this story with the public I served due to its highly embarrassing content, but like I always say, confession is good for the soul, and this story happens to be a prime example.

One of the very first winters I was finally able to cruise around my district without having to commit to a warden's school or some other departmental program, I rode the State-issued snowmobile as much as I possibly could. Doing so provided me with a great opportunity to become better acquainted with many of the more-remote areas of my district. It seemed as though whenever I wanted to take one of these memorable snowmobile journeys, there was always someone available to accompany me on the trip. Many times it was another warden, or occasionally a new acquaintance I'd met along the way.

In February of 1972, I was just recovering from a bout of intestinal flu that had literally knocked me off my feet for a few days. During that time I'd experienced a high fever and a rather serious bout of uncontrollable diarrhea. On this particular morning I was starting to feel somewhat better as compared to the past few days, but I still didn't feel as chipper as I normally did. One of my fellow wardens had called the camp anxiously inquiring if I was available to spend a couple of hours riding snow sleds around the Frye Mountain Game Management Area in the towns of Knox and Montville.

At first I hesitated, saying I didn't really believe I should go off on such a trip because I still didn't feel 100 percent. But with his continued persistence, he eventually persuaded me that the fresh air just might do me some good. We met at the base camp located in Montville, where together we shot up over the mountain on the well-groomed trails. These trails were quite wide and well maintained, allowing us to travel at what we considered then to be breakneck speeds—in those days, a whopping 40 mph, tops, unlike the 110 mph today's machines are capable of traveling.

Also during this particular era, trails that were well-groomed enough to accommodate snow machines were scarce. Various snowmobile clubs were just starting to form, and any plans to initiate a statewide trail system were unthinkable in those days.

I was following close behind my buddy as he led the way around the maze of trails in the management area. Suddenly I was overcome by a series of sharp stomach cramps, just like those I'd experienced in the past few days, when I'd had to make a mad dash to the toilet for quick relief. I knew that time was of the essence. I needed relief. I needed it right then!

Quickly pulling the snow machine over to the side of the trail, I hurriedly shuffled out through the knee-deep snow and underneath the low-hanging branches of a nearby hemlock tree that I hoped would provide some shelter.

By now I was cramping badly; I knew I didn't have a minute to spare. Throwing my helmet off to one side, I desperately lowered my snow-mobile suit and clothing, preparing as best I could for that much-needed relief to follow. In just a few brief seconds I felt much better. Fortunately, I had a handkerchief which I used for a purpose that you can well imagine.

Upon completing my chore, I quickly started to get dressed so that I might return to my snow sled before my partner realized I was gone. He had continued along the trail, unaware that I was no longer behind him.

To this day I don't know why I did it. Maybe it was habit, or perhaps just plain curiosity, but as I stood back up, I happened to turn around to glance at the cause of my discomfort. I reckon it was similar to a cat digging in a litter box, checking to see how good a job it had done after going to the bathroom. Thank God I checked— for in my haste to accomplish the task at hand, the hood on my snowmobile suit had flopped out directly behind and beneath me. There, deposited squarely in the middle of my nice, warm hood, was the entire reason for my emergency stop!

Now what the hell was I going to do? The hood of my snowmobile suit was permanently attached to the suit itself. Certainly I couldn't just dump it out and continue along as if nothing had happened. I had but one choice, and that was to cut the hood off with my jackknife and leave it behind.

It was a small miracle that in my haste to get back out to my machine I hadn't quickly jumped up and pulled the suit—hood included—back into place, dumping the contents squarely down over my head. I think of that old saying—"Go shit in your hat and pull it down over your head"—becoming a stark reality in my case, one that damn near came true.

My buddy, by now realizing that I was no longer tagging along behind him, was returning to my parked sled to see if everything was okay. By then I had managed to cut the hood away from my snowmobile suit and was once again wallowing back out through the deep snow toward my machine. I had left the hood and its contents underneath the hemlock tree.

I didn't dare tell him of my situation. I knew damn well that if I did, the embarrassing experience would quickly spread far and wide. At the moment my little secret was safely locked away in my own mind.

As we continued along on our journey, it was extremely cold riding, especially without the warm hood providing protection from the wind whistling underneath my helmet.

A few days later I made a special trip to the Augusta storehouse, asking Linda Perry, the storehouse clerk, to replace the entire snowsuit with the missing hood. Rather soberly I said, "Linda, the snowmobile suit you folks issued me doesn't have a hood on it like the others. It almost appears as if someone has cut it off."

Staring at the cut-up garment in total amazement, Linda said, "Why to hell would anyone have done that?" I simply shrugged my shoulders and said, "Beats the hell out of me!"

The Day President Reagan Was Shot

On March 30, 1981, John Hinckley Jr. attempted to assassinate President Ronald Reagan. There were folks who probably didn't care much at the time, any more than they do now, but for most of us, this senseless act of violence was a bleak day for the country, executed by a mentally unstable individual operating on a fantasized whim. Regardless of a person's political affiliation, any attempt to permanently silence one of our elected leaders marks a sad chapter in our country's history. Fortunately, President Reagan recovered from Hinckley's attempt to end his life and leadership.

Do you remember where you were or what you were doing on that day? Sadly, many of us wardens had our own tragic situation to deal with, as several of us gathered at Pushaw Lake in an attempt to recover the bodies of two men whose canoe had capsized the previous night. Their canoe had been found floating that morning. The young men were presumed to be somewhere below the surface of this large body of water—the lake was nearly seven miles long—but no one knew exactly where. The ice had melted a few days earlier, which meant the water temperature was such that most people would be incapable of surviving in the lake for very long, especially without life preservers.

Family and friends of the victims had gathered along the shoreline to watch as a small contingent of wardens dragged divers behind their boats in an attempt to locate the missing men. The team of wardens assigned to this task included myself, Sergeant Bill Allen, wardens Terry Glatt, Arnold Beleckis, Bill Pidgeon, Chuck Allen, Parker Tripp, Gary Ballanger, Doug Miner, and the old-timer of the group, Warden Don Gray.

Locating bodies submerged in cold water is a gruesome and difficult task, especially when an exact location is unknown. Sergeant Allen and I were busy stringing buoys across the pond in a straight line to establish some sort of a search area to be covered by the divers, who were slowly and methodically scouring the bottom of the lake. The canoe had drifted for most of the night, and it was anyone's guess as to where they may have capsized.

Our efforts on March 30, 1981, ended in the late afternoon, with no success. Plans were made to continue the operation at daylight the next morning. As we gathered at the boat landing to discuss the strategy for the next day, someone in the group said, "Hey, did you guys hear that someone has shot President Reagan? It's all over the radio. He's been rushed to the hospital and it's unknown if he has survived or not."

I recalled hearing a similar message being broadcast over the loudspeakers at my high school back on November 22, 1963, when Lee Harvey Oswald gunned down John F. Kennedy. I felt a cold chill running up and down my spine, the same feeling that I'd had on that fateful day in 1963. Here we were again, experiencing a time when a man's hate-filled and fantasized rage had reared its ugly head against one of our national leaders.

The morning news was much more positive for the president. He had survived the attempt on his life and was recovering at a Washington, D.C., hospital. So, too, was Secret Service Agent Tim McCarthy and D.C. police officer, Tom Delahanty; both men had taken bullets themselves trying to protect the president. Although gravely wounded, James Brady, Reagan's press secretary, also survived, even though he would spend the rest of his life in a wheelchair.

Meanwhile, the dive team's efforts to retrieve the bodies of the two young men who had ventured out after dark onto a Maine lake without wearing proper flotation devices continued for a second day. Could life jackets have made a difference? No one could honestly say. If nothing else, they would have guaranteed the recovery of the lifeless bodies much sooner.

Sadly, every year, somewhere in our state, the same scenario repeats itself again and again. Many folks still venture out onto the water with the attitude that they are impervious to such fatal circumstances. They wade into danger subconsciously believing it could never happen to them.

Late on the afternoon of March 31, the body of one man was located on the bottom of the lake. The searchers finally had a location on which to concentrate. But once again, the search for the remaining victim had to be discontinued when darkness set in. The last victim was located early the next morning, April 1, 1981, not far from where his buddy's body had been found the day before.

Thus ended a sad chapter for the family and friends of the two young victims, who had somberly huddled along the shoreline, hoping this was nothing more than a bad dream. Unfortunately, it turned out to be a real-life nightmare.

I recorded this sad entry in my diary, hoping it might be the last time I'd log such an incident, but it wouldn't be. There are far too many similar tragedies found within my daily logs. The dive team continues to be active today. This elite group of dedicated wardens is required to perform duties under the most difficult of conditions. They do their jobs admirably and with compassion, never asking for credit or praise, simply performing a service that most folks can't imagine. Once they've completed the dreaded task, they return to their respective districts to perform their daily law enforcement duties, haunted by the gruesome images. It certainly takes a special breed of man to accept this specialized duty, and I take my hat off to them for providing closure for victims' families and friends.

So I ask you again: Do you know where you were the day President Reagan was shot, and do you remember what you were doing?

I recall exactly what I was doing that tragic day. I only wish I didn't remember it quite so well.

Surprise, Surprise

There is one memorable thing about law enforcement work: You never know what to expect, or when to expect it. Such was the occasion one October night in 1977, when, working with my partner Norm Gilbert, I located a vehicle that was well concealed in some bushes at the back end of a remote cornfield in Troy. Being the suspicious creatures that we were, we decided to hide our cruiser and lie in wait, hiding in the brush near the parked vehicle. We hoped to possibly bag an illegal hunter, or perhaps a poacher dragging a deer back to his vehicle.

Sergeant Bill Allen decided to join us on the stakeout.

The daylight was quickly disappearing as we hid well out of sight yet close enough to the car in order to confront anyone returning to it. There was no reason for this vehicle to be hidden in this area other than whomever it belonged to was up to some deviltry that needed a little legal attention.

As dusk quickly settled into darkness, we patiently waited in the brush, wondering what the conclusion of this latest stakeout might bring. This area was noted for its abundance of deer; in fact, a few nights earlier, I'd spotted a big buck grazing underneath one of the apple trees surrounding the cornfield, sporting one of the largest racks I'd ever seen. In the past, I'd received complaints of rifle shots coming from this area just after dark. It was obvious someone else was aware of this remote cornfield surrounded by apple trees, and they'd been taking full advantage of it.

It was a bit difficult for the three of us to stand quietly in the woods without speaking, coughing, belching, or making any noise whatsoever, but we managed. I'd been on similar stakeouts before, only to have some duo return to their car after having been off on a romp elsewhere. Some of these folks were highly respectable citizens engaged in a little secretive adultery—people who didn't want to be seen together and suspected of being on a romantic rendezvous. Could this be one of those times?

The minutes slowly turned into hours. It got darker, and still, the vehicle remained hidden in the brush with no one around. Maybe it was a stolen car, ditched in this remote spot to remain undetected? Lord knows there were plenty of incidents like this happening throughout the state.

We whispered softly between us, listening to sounds from the community. Vehicles could be heard off in the distance as they traveled freely up and down the main highway leading from Unity village to Dixmont and beyond. Bill and Norman were getting a bit restless, wondering if perhaps we weren't sitting there for nothing; perhaps no one would return to the abandoned vehicle, and thus we were simply wasting our precious time.

"Let's give it another half-hour," I whispered. "If they don't come back by then, we'll run a check on the vehicle and get to hell out of here!" I had a gut feeling there was a reason why we'd come into this area, and I wanted to follow up on it. Rather reluctantly, they both agreed.

We remained hunkered down in the bushes, flashlights at the ready just in case we needed to illuminate the area or use them to defend ourselves. Suddenly Norman said, "Did you hear that?"

"Hear what?" I inquired.

"I just heard the cracking of sticks and what sounded like footsteps coming up through the woods where that snowmobile trail comes out into the field," he said. That was one thing about the old boy: There certainly wasn't anything wrong with his hearing, unless of course he wanted there to be. If he chose not to hear you, then you could scream at the top of your lungs and he'd just keep on looking straight ahead.

Suddenly we heard the voices of a couple of

men deep in conversation, coming up the nearby snowmobile trail. We couldn't see them, but they were obviously heading our way.

"Wait until they're almost on top of us before you make a move," Bill suggested. We all nodded in agreement. Not knowing what to expect next, I could feel the adrenaline rushing into my veins. We could barely make out the two figures slowly walking along the edge of the field, both of them coming our way. They appeared to be carrying something over their shoulders.

Thump thump thump . . . Their footsteps ground into the dirt as they closed in on our location. It was show-and-tell time. "Let's get 'em!" I shouted.

The still air was shattered by flashing lights and the screams of "Game wardens—hold it right there!" Those guys couldn't have run if they'd wanted to. We scared the ever-living bejeezus out of them as we scurried in their direction, demanding that they drop the two pillowcases of items hoisted high up on their shoulders. I recognized one of the young men as a local hoodlum who'd been in trouble with the law several times before. His accomplice was a young fellow I had come to know, someone I never would've expected to be involved in any illegal shenanigans.

It turned out that our suspected poachers

weren't poachers after all. Instead, they'd hiked through the woods on the snowmobile trail, breaking into several nearby houses. They were stealing jewelry, VCRs, radios, booze, money, and anything else they could carry in their overstuffed pillowcases (and even those were stolen).

That night may not have ended with another notch added to my flashlight, indicating an apprehended poacher, but it sure did bring a big sigh of relief to those residents living nearby.

With the thieves secured, Maine State Police trooper Richard Reitchel was summoned to prosecute and handle the violation. In the process he was able to solve several other recent burglaries that had taken place in the region that until now had left police baffled, with no suspects whatsoever.

Although I'm sure these young thieves had felt safe as they approached their getaway vehicle, the shocked expressions on their faces indicated otherwise as they stood in handcuffs, waiting for the Maine State Police trooper to haul them off to the county slammer.

Memorial Day Memories

It seems as though every Memorial Day, I find myself visiting the Maine Law Enforcement Officers' Memorial located in Augusta, Maine, where the names of several officers who have made the ultimate sacrifice are neatly carved into the polished granite stone. Several of these are the names of personal friends I've known over the years.

One of the first to be listed upon the polished stone was the name of a warden pilot who left an impression on me when I was just seven years old. He offered me the experience of a lifetime by taking me on my first flight up into the wild blue yonder. It wasn't in a commercial aircraft by any means; instead, it was a spur-of-the-moment deal when my brother, who was four years older than me, and I were invited into the cockpit of a small Piper Cub aircraft piloted by game warden George Townsend of Rangeley.

George was a friend of the family. During the winter months, he frequently came to southern Maine to fly the wardens in the area as they searched for the various illegal activities happening within their districts. When in southern Maine, George stored the drums of aviation fuel for his plane in our backyard. During the night, he left the aircraft anchored on the ice of Mousam Lake a short distance from our home.

One afternoon as my brother and I were skating, George buzzed the treetops and slowly glided down onto the ice a short distance away from us. As he pulled up to the shoreline, he motioned for us to come over.

"How would you boys like to go for a little flight?" he asked.

I don't have to tell you how excited I was as I climbed into that airplane, ice skates and all. We quickly shot out across the pond and up into the air. It was a moment that I'll cherish forever. I can still remember it as clearly today as when it happened, some fifty-four years ago. It was such a thrill to have George coming into the area, especially when he made a low-level pass over our house in the red-and-yellow Piper Cub, signaling for us to come down to the pond to pick him up. Just being able to get near the fascinating flying machine was a treat in itself, let alone even thinking about getting a ride.

During the summer months, our family ventured to the Rangeley area for vacation. We would meet up there with George, his wife, Louise, and their two sons, Craig and David. Craig was my age, and David was the same age as my brother. Being typical boys, we chummed around together and somehow managed to get into the mischief that young boys so often find.

Sadly, on August 27, 1956, George Townsend and a department biologist were taking off from Maranacook Lake in Winthrop in a new Cessna floatplane, when suddenly a pin holding the pilot's seat failed, abruptly causing the seat to slide backwards. This action caused George to lose control of the plane. It fell back into the water, killing both George and his passenger. Needless to say, it was a horrible tragedy for the department and the many friends George had made during his tenure as a Maine game warden. Hardly a Memorial Day passes that I don't recall that cold winter afternoon when I experienced my first flight, and the man who piloted the plane.

Many years later, I was offered another flight in a warden's plane, this time by Warden Pilot Richard Varney, of Readfield. Dick had scheduled a flight with my mentor, warden Vernon Walker of Springvale, and they'd asked if I'd like to tag along. I thought to myself, *Does a bear poop in the woods?! Damn tootin' I'd like to go!* By then I was a young teenager with the desire of hopefully becoming a game warden myself.

Like George Townsend, Richard Varney was another professional, a man with a great personality and attitude. He'd do anything for anybody, and he was second to none in his skills as a pilot.

I finally achieved my goal in 1970, donning my uniform as the state's newest game warden. Soon afterward, Dick flew onto Unity Pond to pick me up. Together we went aloft, searching high overhead in my new district, trying to learn the geography of the area together.

Tragically, on September 27, 1972, Richard Varney also died on Maranacook Lake in Winthrop, when the engine failed on the helicopter he was piloting. The failure caused it to crash back into the water. Dick drowned while trying to escape the flying machine. His name is now inscribed on the officers' memorial in Augusta as yet another fallen comrade who made the ultimate sacrifice.

Both of these men were heroes in my book. Both of them lost their lives in the line of duty, doing what they loved most: flying over the great state of Maine while providing a service to sportsmen. I often think of the pleasant memories I'd shared with these men—two professionals who helped this youngster achieve his own dream of one day working for the sportsmen of Maine.

Another name on the memorial is that of Maine state trooper Charles Black. Tragically, Trooper Black was gunned down by two men on July 9, 1964, during a bank robbery in the small Maine town of South Berwick. Trooper Black was getting a haircut next door to the Maine National

Bank in South Berwick when the robbery occurred. Running outside to investigate the commotion, he was shot in cold blood and left mortally wounded on the sidewalk. I was seventeen at the time, and it just so happened that I was only a few miles away from the scene when this terrible incident occurred. I still remember the roadblocks and the many police cars screaming into the area as the police searched for the two crooks. They were later captured in New Hampshire and convicted. Trooper Black was another hero who in a moment's notice had made the ultimate sacrifice.

The name of Trooper Thomas Merry also appears on the memorial. I had the pleasure of working with this associate in blue, whose patrol area was adjacent to my own. On July 12, 1980, Tom was in the process of setting up a roadblock in Palmyra to stop a motorist who was fleeing from fellow police officers during a high-speed chase. Ironically, this incident happened near the trooper's house. The fleeing hoodlum lost control of his vehicle, striking and killing the young trooper as his wife watched nearby.

Just the day prior to this tragedy, Trooper Richard Reitchel and I had met with Tom at a local restaurant in Unity. We told war stories and shared some quality time together, never suspecting that twenty-four hours later the young officer would be the next in line to make the ultimate sacrifice.

More than seven hundred police officers attended Tom's funeral on a hot summer day in the town of Fairfield. It was a highly emotional tribute, like nothing I'd ever witnessed before. There was hardly a dry eye in the community as a quiet but steady stream of police cruisers and flashing blue lights followed the hearse carrying Tom's body to a nearby cemetery.

Further down the list is the name of game warden William Hanrahan. Bill was a fellow officer working within my division, a dedicated warden who was fearless in his pursuit of poachers and violators. He was also one of the first wardens to acquire a K-9 to aid him with his duties. On November 21, 1992, Bill and his dog, Major, were investigating a report of drunken hunters in the woods. After running a track, they returned to the warden's truck where Bill suffered a massive heart attack and died at the age of forty-two. His death was yet another tragic blow to the department, not to mention the total devastation it brought to those of us who knew him so well. Bill's name is proudly inscribed on the officers' memorial, as well it should be.

These are only a few of the great heroes I find myself thinking about every Memorial Day. Each one has a special place in my memories, and sadly, each of them made the ultimate sacrifice, doing what they enjoyed the most.

There is one more name that I feel should have been included on the list of fallen heroes, but for some reason it wasn't: the name of my good friend, Sheriff Robert M. Jones of Unity. Bob died of a massive heart attack on his birthday, January 12, 2000, while assisting the Unity Fire Department at the scene of a fatal fire that also claimed the lives of three seven-year-old autistic children. Even though my friend's name may not appear on the officers' memorial, he'll forever remain a hero in the eyes of those of us who knew him and were aware of the circumstances surrounding his untimely death. He also died doing what he loved the most—serving the citizens in his community.

Memorial Day is always a solemn occasion when we should take the time to reflect upon the men and women who have died either fighting for our country, or fighting to preserve the peace and safety of the rest of us here at home. Whenever I pass the Maine Law Enforcement Officers' Memorial in Augusta, I always think of the many members within my own profession who gave their all, especially those with whom I shared a personal acquaintance. The Maine Warden Service up until this time had fourteen members who died in the line of duty, listed on the memorial—the highest of any profession in the state's law enforcement field. May their memories forever be preserved in the granite stone for the great sacrifices they've made.

Where Was Kate When I Needed Her?

February of 1978 was a very emotional and tense month, in more ways than one.

I was reviewing my daily logs shortly after reading my friend Kate Braestrup's best-selling book, *Here If You Need Me.* Her book recounted a real-life adventure in which she dealt with her Maine State Police trooper husband's tragic death and then became the Maine Warden Service chaplain.

Today, Kate provides spiritual guidance to wardens and their families dealing with tragedy, helping them cope with the severe emotions they've suddenly had thrust upon them.

There were a few times I could have really used her services, especially following the events of February 11, 1978, when I responded to a serious snowmobile accident in Troy—an accident that involved a young child.

Snowmobiles were just beginning their rise in popularity. More trails were being created, and the machines were capable of traveling much faster than the little snowdrift-hopper I'd been issued.

The dreaded thought of responding to a

mishap involving one of these mechanical monsters was a bummer at best, although the department had been preparing us for such events. The agency had predicted these incidents would become a normal part of our duties as the popularity of these machines increased. The thought of a child being involved didn't help matters any as I hastened toward the scene.

I could hear the local rescue squad being paged out to the call as I shot through Unity, headed for Troy. It was somewhat reassuring to know I wouldn't be alone in my efforts, as I silently hoped the injuries were not life-threatening.

Within minutes, I arrived at the site only to find that a snowmobile collision was not the cause of the tragedy. Instead, two young child-hood buddies had been sliding together on a toboggan adjacent to the rural country road. One of them had managed to jump off the speeding snow sled just before it shot up over the high snowbank, plunging directly into the path of an oncoming car.

His little friend wasn't so lucky.

As I pulled up to the area, the parked car was precariously perched in the middle of the road, with people frantically scurrying about. They were hugging and desperately trying to console each other in what appeared to be a case of sheer pandemonium.

I could see the back of the toboggan wedged under the rear tires of the vehicle, with the legs of a young child lying motionless on top.

The ambulance pulled in directly behind me, which in itself was a relief. But the valiant efforts of the rescue personnel were too late. It was obvious the eleven-year old boy was deceased.

No person is ever totally prepared for such a tragedy. It was total chaos. The driver of the vehicle needed medical care as he was slipping into shock, screaming that he hadn't had any warning of the impending collision.

Immediately, I requested the Maine State Police to dispatch a trooper to the scene to cover this incident, as it fell within their authority. Trooper Stan Cunningham was assigned to cover the tragedy, assisted by his sergeant, James Nolan. I stood by to help them in whatever way I could.

I was personally familiar with this victim's family, which made the incident all the more difficult. I'd recently joined the Masonic Lodge with the young boy's dad a few weeks earlier. During that time we had become friends.

Someone from the area, with good intentions, but obviously not much forethought, called the father, requesting him to come to the scene immediately.

The horrible sight of a distraught dad witnessing

the terrible tragedy inflicted upon his only child truly broke my heart as I furiously fought back my own tears. Dad had to be physically restrained from climbing underneath the car and cuddling his son one last time.

The boy's mom, who was on a shopping trip in Bangor, was expected to be driving down the same highway at any moment, completely unaware of the tragedy.

Trooper Cunningham was a real pro as he went about his business of investigating the tragedy. But it was quite obvious both of us were emotionally drained as we desperately tried to maintain some sense of professionalism and strength during this time of heartbreak.

I recall departing the scene as quickly as I could, thinking of my own son, and imagining how I'd cope under such circumstances as I slowly headed for home.

Once I was far away from the crowd and secure in my own little world, I found myself shedding those pent-up tears of sorrow that I so desperately had fought back while at the scene. I too felt some of that pain and unimaginable grief my friend and his family were enduring.

Little John got a special hug that night. It was one where I simply wanted to hold him close and never let go.

The public has come to expect police officers and investigators to be highly trained and skilled and not show any emotion at such a scene as this, but there's no way a person can ever be trained for such a tragedy. Each situation is different. Every one of them is difficult to deal with, especially when a youngster is involved, and more so when it involves someone you know.

The next few days I visited my friend to offer some sort of personal support, such as it was. Together, we shed many tears, as he and his wife desperately struggled to cope with their unimaginable loss.

For a short period of time, I doubted whether I had the courage and endurance expected of me to continue performing my duties in such horrific circumstances. It certainly was a part of this profession I grew to hate the most, but it also was one that had to be done, and someone had to do it.

During this period the agency had no spiritual support; we simply dealt with these types of issues as best we could.

Life for the boy's family continued, but it would never be the same. The boy's bedroom was left exactly the way it had been when he departed home on that horrific day. Leaving the room undisturbed was the family's way of dealing with a tragedy that would haunt them forever. In the end the two parents split up and went their separate ways. Life for them was never again the happy and joyous occasion it once was.

As for me, although I've experienced my fair share of tragedies over the years, none would bother me more than this one. For some reason, I couldn't seem to get it out of my mind, and even today I find myself getting those same cold chills and shedding a few tears, just thinking about it. I look back and can only ask myself, "Where was Kate when I needed her?"

Jimmy and the Ice Chisel

The winter months required us wardens to check the beaver flowages, making sure the beaver trappers were conforming to the state laws.

Trapping regulations stipulated no beaver traps were to be placed closer than twenty-five feet from a beaver house, or closer than ten feet from a beaver dam. These rules were adopted to prevent a colony of beaver from being eradicated as they conducted their daily routines beneath the frozen surface. The trapping law also required every trap to be properly labeled with the owner's name and address.

A warden was expected to venture onto the ice of a flowage, checking around the beaver houses and dams and measuring the distances where any traps were placed. In those cases of non-compliance, we were authorized to seize the traps as evidence and to write a summons for the owner.

In order to seize these traps, we needed an instrument capable of chopping through the thick ice. The department provided no tool to perform this task, thus leaving it to the individual warden to devise his own means of securing an ice chisel or an ax in order to dig out the traps set well below the thick layers of ice.

In the late winter of 1977, my buddy, Jimmy Ross, the newest addition to the warden force, met up with me on a beaver flowage located in the town of Clinton. Jimmy's new district covered the nearby Skowhegan area which was just to the north of my normal patrol area.

I'd found a couple of illegally set traps placed too close to the beaver house, and I was chiseling my way through the thick ice to remove them when Jimmy arrived at my location. We made some small talk between us. I was proud to see my young friend embarking upon his new career with the same enthusiasm I myself had years before.

"Damn, that's a nice-looking chisel you've got. Where'd you get it?" Jimmy inquired, as I continued slicing through the thick ice, seeking the illegal trap below.

With a devious smirk on my face I said, "I picked it up yesterday at the department's storehouse in Augusta. Linda, the storage clerk, only has a couple of them left. She won't pass them out to just any warden. You really have to beg and force the issue for her to give you one. Matter of fact, she'll probably deny having them, so you want to be quite persistent," I maliciously fibbed to my little buddy, knowing damn well that she never had such an item.

In essence, I was setting Jimmy up to see if he'd go to Augusta demanding a chisel just like mine from the ferocious "tiger lady" who ran the department's storehouse as if it was a maximum-security unit at a federal prison.

Linda was definitely one of a kind. She was a rather tall, large-boned, muscular lady, who towered high above most of the wardens standing alongside of her. Her size alone proved to be quite intimidating, and she conveniently took advantage of it. Linda operated the storehouse as an extremely tight ship in regards to getting any equipment or supplies from her. It was her decision and hers alone as to what you got and what you didn't. It was a decision that few wardens dared to challenge.

To put it mildly, most wardens were petrified of the Amazon lady who operated the State-owned supply shed like a drill sergeant in the Marine Corps. God forbid if anyone tried to scam her and she ever found out about it. There would be hell to pay. Linda had the memory of an elephant; she never forgot, and she always managed to get even.

Over the past few years, I'd been rather fortunate. For some strange reason, we'd developed a friendly relationship between us, one where I could get just about anything I ever wanted with very little effort and a whole lot of sweet-talking. Now I have to admit, sweet talk was something I was good at, especially when it was needed the most.

I recall returning my snowmobile suit after having had an embarrassing accident involving the hood. I had been forced to cut the hood off the garment with my pocketknife, thus rendering the suit completely useless.

Linda had doggedly questioned the circumstances surrounding the event when I swapped the suit for another, but I simply convinced her it had been a defective suit to begin with. I knew damn well she thought otherwise, but she pushed no further for a full explanation (thank God).

Jimmy was quite excited as to how quickly I was slicing through the ice with my brand-new chisel. Although I'd purchased it the day before at a local hardware store in Unity, Jimmy was thoroughly convinced that Linda was issuing these chisels at the storehouse.

I fully intended to tell him the difference before we parted company that day, but as time passed, I forgot.

It was an honor to have my pal, Jim, working alongside me, especially now that he was serving the department in an official capacity. Without a doubt, his future with the agency would be highly successful, just as long as he didn't argue and show that independent streak of resisting changes in the department's operational procedures—something I was guilty of.

Together we spent the rest of the morning

confiscating a few more illegal beaver sets and tracking down the violators. At the conclusion of our business, we went our separate ways. Before he left, Jim stated he was heading for Augusta. "Perhaps we can meet up again a little later on in the week and find some more," he said enthusiastically.

As I drove off, I thought of how I'd forgotten to tell Jim the real truth about where my chisel had come from. Oh well, it was no big deal; I'd fill him on the details the next time we met.

Later that evening I received a phone call from my little buddy. "You #$@%*&!" Jim cursed and carried on over the telephone.

"What the heck are you all fired up about?" I asked.

"The chisel, the chisel," Jimmy screamed. Suddenly it dawned on me that he must've done the inevitable. He had been in and asked the "tiger lady" for a chisel!

"You didn't ask Linda for a chisel, did you?" I shouted.

"What the hell do you think!" he yelled. "I walked into the storehouse and told Linda that I wanted to be issued one of those ice chisels she had secretly tucked away in the back room," Jim said disgustedly.

"Just like you told me, she denied having them. So, I pursued the issue a little harder—just like you said to," he sputtered. "She got madder and madder, but I held my ground, thinking that at any minute she'd give in and go get me the damned thing. But oh no, I pushed her to the point of where she was about ready to climb up over the counter and throttle me," he said. "Damn you! You set me up, didn't you?" he shouted.

"It wasn't until I finally told Linda where I'd come up with all of this ice-chisel bull-crap that she cracked a smile and calmed down." He chuckled.

"I don't think I'd hurry back to the storehouse real soon, John Boy," said Jim. "I think the Queen Bee is anxiously awaiting your return in a big way.

"Oh, and by the way, she kept asking me about a snowmobile suit you'd returned a while back —something to do with the hood missing off of it?

"I didn't know you'd never told her the truth of how you'd crapped in it and then cut it off with your knife," he said, chuckling, "but that's okay, John Boy. I filled her and everybody else who was there in on the truth of the missing hood." Jimmy snickered. "It was the least I could do."

It looked like my little chisel caper might have backfired. I guess that old saying of, "What goes around comes around!" is true.

I definitely deserved what I had coming to me.

A Better Use of the Finger

Those of us in law enforcement often witnessed the use of the almighty finger whenever approaching a suspect or a person whose opinion of the man behind the badge wasn't always the most complimentary. That middle-finger salute didn't particularly signal that we were number one in the flipper's book by any means.

Unlike the defiant culprits who used their fingers to send a personalized message to those of us in uniform, I recall a time when my finger actually brought about a satisfactory conclusion to a man-on-the-run incident.

It was in the wee hours of a March morning in 1984 when I was awakened by a phone call from Maine State Police requesting assistance in a high-speed chase that had originated in the city of Waterville, quite some distance away. The suspect appeared to be heading toward Brooks, with a whole flotilla of police cruisers bobbing along in pursuit. The entourage included several units from the Maine State Police, the Fairfield Police, Waterville Police, and the Waldo County sheriff's office.

Rolling out of bed, I quickly donned my gear. As I shot out the door I could hear the parade of blaring sirens flying through town a mile or so away, screeching along Main Street in pursuit of the young fellow and then careening onto a back road leading out of the village.

The vehicle was registered to a local man with whom I was very familiar. Benny (not his real name) lived with his mother near the village. From the direction of travel, it appeared as though Benny was trying to shake off the hounds that were hot on his trail and make it back home. No one was saying why he was on the run, but knowing Benny, it was more than likely a drunk-driving charge.

As I sped into the village, I heard an officer yell over the radio, "He's plowed into a snowbank and has bailed out of his vehicle. Now he's high-tailing it through the woods. We'll be following his tracks out through the deep snow!"

I notified them that I was well aware of Benny's home base, and I was headed there now. I'd simply position myself in an area where I could watch the house, which more than likely was his final destination. Hiding my vehicle a short distance away, I scurried down along the narrow road in front of Benny's residence and took up surveillance behind a large pine tree located not far from the front of the house. There was a heavy layer of snow in the woods, as it had been a long winter.

Waldo County deputy Steve Drake and Maine

State Police trooper Greg Morse were hot on Benny's trail, waddling waist-deep in the snow, trying to catch the fleeing felon. None of them were prepared for the chase, floundering through the thick brush and deep snow without the aid of snowshoes.

On the other hand, I was quite comfortable snuggled in behind the pine tree, just biding my time. I surmised that Benny would eventually make his appearance—that is, if they didn't tackle him beforehand. After several minutes of patiently waiting and listening, I heard someone huffing and puffing, heading my way. I simply leaned back against the tree, intently watching the woods around me.

Before long, I saw Benny struggling along in the deep snow. He was feverishly trying to put some distance between himself and the trail of human bloodhounds not far behind. The adrenaline rush was unbelievable: My heart pounded as I contemplated what action I'd take, and what the next few minutes might bring. There was one thing I could always count on in my profession, and that was plenty of excitement.

As Benny got closer and closer, it was obvious he was about to break out of the woods right beside the pine tree that was providing my cover. From my prior dealings with Benny I knew that once he was cornered, he wasn't noted for being violent or resisting arrest. But this situation seemed far more serious than any of the others I had previously encountered. I couldn't imagine why he was working so hard to evade the officers; was this a simple traffic violation, or had he committed some other atrocity? The reason for making the stop still hadn't been communicated by those involved in the chase. (I later learned that Benny and his friend had consumed one too many beers and had chosen not to submit to an imminent arrest. They decided to try to out-run the cops, hoping to lose them along the way.)

There he was, a few feet away, desperately lifting his short little legs up and down in the deep snow, still managing to maintain some space between himself and his pursuers. Every so often, he'd glance back to see if they were gaining on him.

It was show-and-tell time. As Benny reached my location, I quickly pressed my outstretched finger into the side of his head and screamed, "Hold it right there, Benny! The jig's up!" There was no doubt he believed I had my firearm pointed firmly against his skull. He started screaming, "Don't shoot! Don't shoot! I give up!" It was almost comical to watch as he dove spread-eagle on the ground. He landed by my feet and shook like an old dog passing razor blades. A quick snap of the handcuffs around his wrists subdued him. We both stood up and leaned against the pine tree, awaiting the pursuing officers, who by then were just coming into view.

Within minutes, Steve and Greg arrived at our location, exhausted from the chase. They marched Benny to the waiting squad car for the brief ride to the Waldo County Crowbar Hotel. I, on the other hand, headed back home where I crawled back into bed after spending yet another exciting night beneath the heavens.

In this instance, the loaded finger worked quite well. It was, by far, a better use of a digit than what Benny would have exhibited had the chance presented itself.

Just Another Day
(Walter's Story)

My colleague and good friend, Trooper Mark Nickerson, routinely ended his shift with the same old caption: "Just another day." I'd like to reflect on some of those memorable times that my trooper friend and I shared together, patrolling the same areas. We often seemed to find ourselves mixed up in one catastrophe or another before the day was through.

Take, for instance, the time when I was relaxing in the peace and seclusion of my home, minding my own business, creating a wildlife drawing for the latest edition of *The Sportsman's Calendar*, which I produced annually. This project provided a welcome retreat away from the public, using my creative energy for a positive end. Fellow artists can relate as to how you have to be in the right frame of mind when you are creating. You need a time and space free of interruption and outside influences that could break the thought process required to produce a masterpiece.

On this particular morning as I sat at my kitchen table, peacefully entrenched in my own little world, I glanced up to see my buddy's State Police cruiser pull into my dooryard. Trooper

Nickerson was seated behind the wheel. He quickly parked within the confines of my garage and barged through the door, sporting the devious grin I'd seen so many times in the past.

"What the hell are you smirking about?" I calmly inquired.

"I just saw your buddy, Walter, downtown. He gave me the usual one-fingered salute we always get whenever we meet." Mark chuckled. "Even though it's early in the morning, I'd say he's already been into the booze and is half-pickled."

Walter had become a routine customer for Mark and me. It seemed as though we confronted this man—who despised all cops and anyone in authority—on a daily basis. Whenever our paths crossed, it was a pretty sure bet that Walter was involved in some sort of violation. Rumors were circulating that even though Walter hadn't been known to be violent in the past, he did at one point try to recruit some local thugs to perform a drive-by shooting at my house. As a result, there was a certain animosity between us, comparable to a couple of sparks ready to jump at each other.

Before I could respond to my pal, who by now was seated comfortably at my kitchen table, I looked outside to see Walter screaming into my dooryard on two wheels, in his girlfriend's car. She was behind the wheel as Walter staggered out of the passenger side.

"What the hell did you do to Walter?" I asked

Mark. "He's coming to the door, and he looks madder than a dog with a bad case of rabies!" Needless to say, my morning of peace and quiet was about to be flushed down the crapper in one giant swoop.

Walter marched up to my kitchen door with daggers in his eyes. "Why is that that gawddamned State Police cruiser parked in your garage?" he demanded from the doorstep.

I bluntly replied, "It's none of your gawddamned business what's in my garage, Walter. What do you want?"

Mark was tucked in behind my kitchen door, saying, "Tell him to leave or else he'll be arrested!"—like I really needed someone advising me of the law at that point. As politely as I could, I stated, "Walter, unless you have some official business, which I know you don't, I want you to leave my property immediately." I might just as well have been whispering inside a raging tornado. He never heard a word I said, or at least, he wasn't paying attention.

"I'm a tax-paying citizen of this state," Walter shouted, "and I demand to know why that #$@%*& cruiser is parked in your garage!" His voice could have been heard in Dixmont, some eight miles away.

"Like I told you before, Walter, it's none of your business. Now for the last time, you need to reach behind you, grab your scrawny arse in your hands, and get the hell off my property, or else you're going to be arrested." Obviously by now, the sparks were intensifying, and I knew the inevitable was about to happen. My mind-set had gone from one of creative expression to preparing for immediate battle, and the fight was about to begin.

"You can go right straight to hell!" he screamed. "I don't have to leave here until you tell me why that #$@%*& police cruiser is parked in your garage!"

What little patience I'd had was totally gone. I shot out through the kitchen door like a missile being launched from its launcher, grabbed ahold of Walter, and immediately placed him under arrest for criminal trespass. I had made up my mind that two warnings for him to depart my sacred domain had fallen on deaf ears, and there wasn't about to be a third.

We tumbled into the dooryard, with Mark soon joining the fray. Mark quickly secured Walter in handcuffs and stuffed him into the police cruiser, ready for the trip to the Belfast Crowbar Hotel.

By now, Walter's girlfriend and chauffeur was screaming a list of vile obscenities from her car. I recall telling her in no uncertain terms that she had best leave, or she too would be accompanying her boyfriend to the local lockup. She shot out of the driveway like a dragster trying to set a land speed record on a quarter-mile track.

As quickly as my quiet world had been so rudely interrupted, peace suddenly returned as Mark drove out of my driveway, headed for the Waldo County jail with Walter seated next to him. I sat at my kitchen table, stewing over the events of the past few minutes, while at the same time trying to force myself back into working on my wildlife illustration.

Without warning, I suddenly heard Walter screaming obscenities, letting loose a diatribe against Mark and me. I quickly looked outside, thinking for some reason they had returned. I felt my blood boiling all over again.

Mark, apparently not wanting me to miss anything, left his portable radio on my kitchen counter. On their way to the jail, Mark decided to let the outside world hear a version of Walter that we were forced to deal with constantly. He held open the mic of the State Police radio, allowing Walter's tirade to be carried across the airwaves for all of the state to hear. This quickly brought a response from State Police headquarters, who demanded to know if Mark was all set, or if perhaps he needed some assistance. My trooper pal later claimed he didn't know the radio mic was open! Sure, he didn't . . . The boy knew exactly what he was doing, and now I found myself irate all over again.

As I sat there at my kitchen table, I couldn't help thinking about what had happened a couple of days earlier, when I found myself in a similar situation with this moron and his idiotic girl-friend—only this time, Walter was seated next to me in my cruiser, once again in handcuffs.

I happened on this occasion to approach Walter and his girlfriend as she was driving him along a rural highway. As I followed them, I suddenly saw Walter reach over and slap the hell out of his supposed girlfriend. Their car shot from one side of the road to the other. She suddenly slammed on the brakes, leaving the car in the middle of the road and nearly causing a collision between our vehicles.

As she exited the driver's side of the car, she was screaming, "I can't take this anymore!" She had welts around her eyes, and her face was beet red where he had slapped her repeatedly. I quickly stepped in between them, placing him under arrest for assault. Once I got the handcuffs secured and Walter seated inside the cruiser, his girlfriend decided all of a sudden that I was now the villain. She turned on me like a rabid animal. There was no winning with this pair; when they weren't under the influence of alcohol, they were high on drugs. In this case I had little choice but to react as I did. Had I not, I'd have been guilty of neglect for allowing the beating to occur. It was a no-win situation.

On the way to the jail, without warning Walter rolled over on his side and violently kicked at my head. His foot came to rest just inches from the side of my face. Fortunately, he didn't make contact; if he had, we would have been in a major wreck. Needless to say, it wasn't a very pleasant journey for either of us from that point forward.

In the end, the judge sentenced Walter to a short jail term as a result of the criminal trespass charge. He was also ordered to stay out of the town of Brooks for an indefinite period of time. The judge made it perfectly clear that if he saw Walter in his courtroom again in the near future, his days of freely roaming Waldo County would be short-lived. The Big House had a bunk with his name on it, and it would be up to him whether he wanted to use it.

Yup, there was something about patrolling with my trooper buddy, Mark. Seems like each incident we shared was more hair-raising than the last. There was no such thing as "Just another day" when he was around.

Heeeere's Johnny!

Judy was planning on giving us both a Christmas present near the end of 1976, as she was winding down her final month of pregnancy. We still had a few weeks to go (or so we thought) before our family would hopefully increase in size with the arrival of a healthy newborn.

The evening of December 10, 1976, was like any other. I was off working night-hunters in the Unity, Maine, area with my legislative buddy, Ken "Babe" Tozier, keeping me company. Judy had returned home from work a little earlier than usual that day, feeling some discomfort from the baby moving around.

"I've had some fairly sharp pains today. They've been several minutes apart, but I don't think it's anything serious," she said.

"Don't you think maybe I ought to stay home tonight just in case you need to go to the hospital?" I asked nervously.

"Nah, no need to—it's no worse tonight than what it's been before. Besides, the baby isn't due for another week or two, so go ahead and go to work. If I need you, I'll call," she insisted. She was busily munching away on a box of peppermint patties and assorted candies that had arrived in the morning mail as a Christmas gift from a friend. "I'll be fine. I'm going to lie on the couch and watch TV. I'm quite sure the baby will settle down in a little bit," she said reassuringly.

I remained a bit uneasy about leaving her home alone, but the area I intended to work had been heavily hunted the previous few nights, and I felt an obligation to be there too. After all, she was insisting the baby was not due for a few more days, almost indicating she'd rather have a little rest time without my being around. She all but demanded I go to work, and I certainly wasn't about to argue with the queen of the household. (I'd foolishly made that mistake too many times before.)

As Babe and I sat in the cruiser, I jokingly said, "I might have to leave early tonight, Babe. Jude was having some labor pains earlier, but she doesn't think it's anything too serious. She thinks the baby's kicking and banging around like it's done many times before, so it may be nothing at all."

Grinning from ear to ear in the typical Babe fashion that I was so accustomed to, Babe said, "Hee-hee . . . I hope so, for your sake, Fordy. I hope to hell you make out better than I did when our son, Joel, was born."

"Why's that, Babe?" I asked.

"Well, I'll tell ya . . . we started for the hospital in Waterville and made it as far as Unity

Plantation. We were in an area where there were no houses or people around, and the next thing I knew, she groaned a bit, burped once or twice, and had Joel right there in the car."

"Are you serious, Babe? I've never heard that story before!"

"I'm just as serious as I can be," Babe assured me.

"What the hell did you do?" I asked.

"What the hell do you think I did? I helped her as much as I could, wrapped the baby up in a blanket, and then drove like hell for the hospital some twenty miles away. Hee-hee-hee," Babe said, with his trademark snicker.

Babe had just finished telling his story when my mobile radio crackled with a message from the barracks. "You might want to start for your residence ASAP," the dispatcher said. "Your wife is experiencing severe pains and thinks you'd better come home."

My heart climbed up into my throat as I quickly spun out of the driveway we were parked in, heading like a jackrabbit for home port.

I dropped Babe off along the way. "Good luck, Fordy!" he shouted. "Keep me posted."

"I will!" I said, heading for home just as fast as wild horses would go.

Meanwhile, Maine State Police trooper Bruce Dow, who was patrolling near the area, offered his assistance. "I'll swing by your house to make sure she's okay. If she needs to go to the hospital, I'll take her," he reassured me over the radio. Realizing that Bruce was nearby helped ease the tension I was experiencing as I continued toward Brooks at a record pace.

Along the way, I kept thinking of Babe's story, about his wife having the baby in the car. I couldn't help but wonder if perhaps the same damn thing wasn't about to happen to me.

Arriving at the house, I met a nervous trooper in the driveway. "I think you'll be a dad before morning," Bruce said. "Herman is definitely on his way." He chuckled halfheartedly. Our baby had been dubbed "Herman" by the trooper in an effort to make light of the occasion. Bruce didn't seem to want to hang around any too long. "Let me know if you need anything!" he shouted, and with that, he shot out of the driveway like a bullet.

Once inside the house, I found Judy bent over in the living room, in obvious discomfort. I asked her if she had anything packed to take to the hospital, or if she had called our family doctor, Doc Wagner.

"Not yet," she said. "I really don't think we'll need to go tonight," she chirped. As usual, Judy was extremely stubborn when it came to seeing a doctor, and this night wasn't about to be an exception.

With Babe's comments still echoing in my

head, I insisted on calling Doc Wagner at his home. Her pains were three to five minutes apart. The country doc answered the phone in his usual businesslike tone. There was absolutely no personal conversation to be had with the man; he limited any talk strictly to the business at hand and absolutely nothing more.

I explained what was happening with Judy.

"Hmmm, sounds like she's in labor, all right," he said. "You'd better get her to the hospital in Bangor. I'll meet you up there," he said.

That sounded good to me, as Judy was experiencing yet another contraction. It was quite obvious she was in a great deal of pain. Quickly tossing a few items into an overnight bag, we struck out for Bangor with blue lights flashing and an occasional blast from the siren. For me, the trip to Bangor seemed like an eternity, although Judy felt like we got there in record time.

Beads of sweat ran down my face as we made our way into the hospital and to the maternity ward. Judy was quickly shuffled into one of the rooms for preparation as I patiently waited outside. Soon afterward, Doc Wagner entered the maternity ward. His hair was standing on end as if he hadn't taken the time to comb it. He casually greeted me on his way by, disappearing into the room where Judy was being prepped.

After a few minutes he returned. "I think she'll

be delivering tonight, but it'll be a while. I'm going into the back room for a nap. I'll keep checking on her. Go ahead in there with her if you want to," he suggested.

Anxious to see what was happening, I hustled into the room where Judy was lying on a gurney, ready for what the night was about to bring. We chatted between us, joking about Bruce's hasty retreat from our dooryard and Babe's rendition of his wild night when he became a parent. I hadn't dared to tell Jude that story until we were securely in place at the hospital. It had been bad enough for me to keep thinking about it; I didn't need her doing the same on the quick trip north.

Suddenly, she said, "I think I'm going to be sick!"

Now, I have to tell you, if there's one weakness I have, it's being around someone who's about to vomit. Without fail, I'll join them every time. I held up a small bucket as she commenced to discard the peppermint patties she had been munching on all evening. I made every effort to control my own stomach, while at the same time yelling for the nurses to assist us. With no immediate response to my panicked cries, I suddenly began filling a pan of my own. Needless to say, this sudden commotion brought far more help than what I had begged for. It also rather quickly got me evicted from the room altogether.

I was politely told to wait outside, where for the next several hours, I nervously pretended to read magazine after magazine, anxiously waiting for the big moment to arrive.

Doc Wagner periodically checked her progress. "She's doing okay," he mumbled each time as he walked through the waiting room.

Finally, at around 4:30 a.m., I couldn't stand it any longer. I needed a cup of coffee and a light snack. The long wait was taking its toll. I informed the nurses I'd be right back, and headed off to the cafeteria a few floors below.

I was used to being confronted with rather odd situations, and this early-morning hour was no different. I met a strange-acting fellow on the elevator who rather bluntly inquired, "Are you a cop?" all the while intently staring at my warden's uniform.

"Nope, I'm a game warden," I said.

"Oh, wow," he said. "Boy, am I ever glad to meet you!" He started telling me about an experience he'd had in Greenville a few days prior. "This big bull moose came running up to me in my car and was trying to nurse off my thumb," he said, shoving his thumb almost directly into my face. "Yup, he ran right along-side the car, trying to suck my thumb as I tried to drive away."

I quickly concluded that the guy was either high on drugs or completely nuts. Somehow, I sensed it was the latter. When I made no comment regarding his story, he inquired, "Why are you here?"

"My wife's having a baby," I said.

"Oh," he replied. We each grabbed a cup of coffee and a little snack and moved over to a nearby table where we sat down across from each other. We were the only ones in the cafeteria at that hour of the day. The conversation with my newfound friend was extremely strange and hard to follow, but I gave it my best shot—more of an effort to appease him than actually caring what he was talking about. I quickly drank my cup of coffee in an effort to shed this stranger, who by then had seemingly adopted me. He quickly jumped up and followed me back onto the elevator, all the while rambling about something else I couldn't understand.

I stepped off the elevator at the maternity ward, happy to have left him behind. Just as I returned to the waiting room, the public address system alerted Security to be on the lookout for an escapee who had walked away from the psychiatric ward. There was no doubt in my mind who I'd just shared a cup of coffee with. At least he'd appeared to be fairly friendly and harmless, which was a good thing, as he was still on the elevator, heading for parts unknown.

I told a nurse what had happened as I shot out the door to see if I could find out which floor he was heading to. The next few minutes I assisted Security in chasing this man from floor to floor. We finally corralled him in a room as he was attempting to talk to anyone who was willing to listen. I was exhausted and dragged myself back to the maternity ward, where the desk clerk graciously thanked me for assisting their security personnel.

"Thank you, thank you. That poor fellow is in dire need of help," she stated. "Are you Mr. Ford, by any chance?" she inquired.

"I am," I said, wondering how she knew.

"Congratulations, Mr. Ford. Your wife just gave birth to a handsome little boy. In a few minutes you can go in to be with both of them. Your wife and baby are doing just fine," she reassured me, as tears filled my eyes. The biggest moment of my entire life had finally arrived, and I'd missed it.

And thus it was that at a little after 5:00 a.m., on December 11, 1976, John Jr. entered this big world of ours while his father was off chasing an escapee from the psychiatric ward at the Eastern Maine Medical Center. Some things never change. When I took the oath of office and agreed to serve and protect, I never dreamed I'd find myself springing into action during the proudest moment of my life—the birth of my son.

A Night Out with Blinky

All across the nation in the early 1980s, game wardens were beginning to use decoy deer in an effort to capture deer poachers. Maine was no exception. Several court rulings, along with a change in departmental policies, allowed the use of decoy deer by Maine wardens. Strict guidelines were in place as to how these decoys were to be used. A warden was allowed to use a homemade silhouette or a similar device under certain conditions, in an effort to capture those hunters pursuing a deer underneath the beam of a bright light or the dim glow of the moon.

Maine's Fish and Game Department lacked the funds to pay for any of the elaborate devices used in other states, so it was left up to each warden to create his own critter, if they so desired. Unlike the realistic, radio-controlled, full-body mounts used in other states, Maine wardens had to resort to their own ingenuity if they ever hoped to have such a tool.

Aided by deputy wardens Scott and Rod Sienkiewicz, we designed a critter of our own that eventually earned the title of Blinky, named by a prominent Belfast defense attorney after he found himself representing a client or two who had succumbed to the good looks of our masterpiece. Blinky was nothing more than a simple piece of plywood made to look like an adult buck. We mounted a large set of antlers on top of it and attached small glass reflectors as eyes. We then painted the silhouette, hoping to make it look more realistic.

Blinky was placed on a wooden base with a large rat trap and a door spring connected by a pin hooked to the backside of the silhouette. By removing the pin, the spring would pull the deer over should someone shoot at it. The pin was pulled from far away by using the radio controls from my short-lived model-airplane adventure. The radio controls were all that remained of a model airplane I'd spent countless hours building during the winter months, only to have it crash and burn on its maiden flight. There wasn't enough left of my craft to build a small bonfire. (So much for my new hobby.) Although Blinky was a rather crude setup, especially when looking at it up close, we hoped it would work well if presented properly. It surely did its job on more than one occasion.

Blinky was used mostly during bright, frosty moonlit nights during the fall—nights when a serious deer poacher cruised the roads, scanning the fields without the aid of a light, searching for a deer standing all by himself in the moonlight.

These conditions were ideal for a silhouette, enticing the serious deer poacher into thinking their quarry was lurking nearby.

Over the years, Blinky provided some rather humorous and interesting moments—and not all of them were at the hands of deer poachers. One of those times involved a man by the name of Junior and his young son, Nathan. I was very familiar with both of them; in fact, Junior actually plowed my driveway during the winter months.

It was late in the evening when they passed by our location shortly after we'd placed Blinky out in a field not too far from where they lived. Junior was a real giant of a man, standing over six feet tall and weighing close to 300 pounds or more. He was a little slow in his actions and spoke with a mild stutter of sorts, but overall he was as gentle as a lamb, despite his intimidating size.

Apparently as they passed by our location on this bright, moonlit night, they glanced out into the field where they saw Blinky standing several feet away. Junior quickly pulled his vehicle over to the edge of the road, coming to a screeching halt. Neither Junior nor Nathan was an avid hunter, so I didn't expect they'd be up to anything illegal. Instead, they exited their vehicle, slowly walking over to the opposite side of the road facing Blinky. Junior began jumping up and down, loudly clapping his hands and hollering and screaming at the plywood statue.

"Shoo, shoo! You g-g-get the hell out of here!" His actions were an obvious attempt to scare the deer out of the field. But as expected, Blinky just stood there in the moon glow, staring back at them. Scott and I were tucked in the bushes a few feet away, watching and listening to their every move. We were desperately trying to maintain our composure at the comical sight we were witnessing.

"Shoo! You damn fool, g-g-get the hell out of here before s-s-someone comes along and shoots you! Shoo, shoo! Get the hell out of here!" Junior continued hollering at Blinky, trying to get him to move along. By now, he was leaping higher up into the air at what seemed almost Olympic heights, all the while screaming and clapping his hands at the deer silhouette nearby.

Nathan just stood there watching the show as his bulky father continued jumping up and down in the roadway, screaming at poor old Blinky off in the distance. Not getting the results they'd hoped for, they both began throwing rocks as far out into the field as possible, trying to scare Blinky away. But still, Blinky never moved a muscle.

Finally, in total desperation and disgust, Junior stuttered, "N-N-Nathan, you go out there and s-s-see what the hell is the matter with that foolish d-d-deer. Make him move on, the damn fool; he's gonna g-g-get shot!" he said.

Being an obedient son, Nathan slowly hoofed it out across the field heading straight for Blinky. Junior just stood in the roadway, watching as Nathan hiked out to where Blinky was situated. After what seemed like an eternity, Nathan finally sauntered up to within three feet of the silhouette. He slowly commenced walking all around it, looking it up and down, but he never once uttered a word back to his father. It was almost as if he was completely speechless.

Junior just stood there, staring intently off into the field. I'm sure he was wondering just what the heck was going on. Ever so slowly, Nathan returned, occasionally stopping along the way to turn around and glance back at Blinky, while shaking his head from side to side in total disbelief. Neither one of them spoke a word as they both just shook their heads, climbed back into their vehicle, and slowly drove away.

A few days after the hunting season ended, we received our first snowstorm. Junior as usual made several passes with his snowplow, clearing my driveway. I invited him to come inside when he finished, intending to pay him for his efforts and offer him a cup of coffee. As we sat at the table talking, I couldn't resist bringing up the incident with Blinky.

"Junior," I said, "you and Nathan didn't happen to run across a dumb deer not too far from your house, in the middle of the night late last fall, did you?"

A silly smirk came across Junior's face, almost as if he'd just solved the crime of the century.

Popcorn, Moxie, and a Wet Hat

Even today, when the frosty fall air invades the countryside, I wish I was spending the cold nights setting beneath the full moon and the bright stars, patiently waiting for that dastardly night-hunter to meander into my sights. Those certainly were good times, shared with a working partner as we talked about everything from raising potatoes to the sex life of everyone within the community and beyond.

During those late nights sitting in the dark, I really enjoyed munching on a bag of store-bought popcorn and a variety of other unhealthy snacks, washing it all down with bottles of Moxie, a Maine specialty, or consuming endless cups of hot coffee. This routine was part of the nightly ritual, and the way life should be.

One evening, Bill Livezey, a young student from Unity College, was riding with me. At that time Bill had high hopes of becoming a game warden, a goal he eventually reached. We were perched underneath a grove of apple trees located on Ward Hill Road in Troy, watching the fields around us and patiently waiting for a ruthless bunch of poachers to venture our way.

It was a dark, cold, and frosty night as we sat snuggled in the comfort of my cruiser with the heater running to keep us warm. I decided it was time for my nightly snack of popcorn, accompanied by a big bottle of that special tingling brew, Moxie. Bill was busy munching away on the sweets he had brought along for his late-evening snack. Carefully opening and reaching into the bag of popcorn, I began swiping at its contents like there was no tomorrow. I could easily consume an entire bag of popcorn in a record number of minutes. I simply thrived on the taste of that heavily buttered and salted popcorn, capped off with a big swig of Moxie to wash it down the hatch.

Reaching into the bag of popcorn I felt something tickling the back of my hand. I just assumed it was a ripped-off portion of the cellophane bag brushing up against my paw as I pulled out a handful of popcorn, so I thought nothing more about it. Bill and I were discussing the usual topics—everything from school activities to sexual promiscuity on campus. It seemed as though no matter who I was working with, the conversation would usually turn to sex in one form or another. (I later learned the popularity of this topic wasn't just due to my own warped fascination; it was the same with many of my brothers in uniform. It's a man's thing, I reckon!)

As I listened to Bill chattering away, I kept reaching into my bag of popcorn, scooping out yet another fistful, thoroughly enjoying every mouthful. I continued to feel that tickling on the back of my hand as I slowly removed the popcorn from the bag. Like so many times before, I simply assumed it was the bag brushing against my skin. Finally, as I reached into the nearly empty bag, the tickling sensation remained on the top of my hand when I pulled it out. It felt like something crawling up my hand toward my arm.

"What the hell . . . ," I said to Bill as I turned on the interior light of my cruiser. Much to my horror, I observed a huge—and I mean, *huge*—black and yellow spider firmly locked onto the back of my hand. His abdomen was severely shrunken and completely covered with a thick layer of yellow dust from the butter and salt of the bagged popcorn. Obviously he'd been trapped inside the bag at the plant and had come along for the ride. For what little time I observed him, he didn't appear to be very healthy.

I let out a profoundly-laced blat that I'm sure scared the bejeezus out of every deer within ten miles of where we were parked. Admittedly, spiders and I are not the fondest of buddies. I quickly launched the bug out through the open window and into the field, just as far away from my cruiser as feasibly possible. Poor Bill was having all he could do trying to contain himself (the sick SOB). With the dome light shining brightly into what remained of the popcorn bag, I frantically searched through the contents, wondering if perhaps Mr. Spider didn't have a relative accompanying him on his journey.

"You don't think there might have been others in the bag and you've already eaten them, do you?" Bill asked with a glint in his eye. The mere thought of this possibility made me quite nauseous. Suddenly what had started out to be a great evening wasn't quite so good. It kind of reminded me of a situation I found myself in many years before, concerning a cup of coffee I shared with an elderly couple in South Unity as their damned cats gave me the evil eye.

Just what was that scratching in the back of my throat? Oh God, you don't suppose . . . Where was my Moxie?

To top off the evening, I found myself in yet another fine mess of sorts, although I'm a little embarrassed to discuss it. After consuming the rest of my large bottle of Moxie, hoping to wash away any foreign objects that might be lodged in my throat, I eventually had to relieve myself. Stepping outside of the cruiser in the dark of the night, I started ridding myself of all the fluid I had consumed. Bill was still chuckling over the spider episode as I stood beside the cruiser, taking care of business. I was busily engrossed in relieving myself when I happened to notice a dark object lying alongside the cruiser on the ground. In a rather childish frame of mind, I took aim at the object and proceeded to cover it with my own bodily fluids. I was climbing back into the cruiser when curiosity got the best of me. Wanting to see what the dark object was, I flashed my light onto it.

There, lying on the ground, was my warden's hat. It had apparently fallen from the cruiser as I made my exit. *Oh, great!* Not only had I eaten what might have been a bag full of spiders, but now I'd urinated on my uniform hat! I wished that Norman, my old working partner, had been there with me instead of Bill. I would've just switched hats with him and never told him the difference.

Seeing how things weren't going so well, I said, "Billy boy, I think it's time to call it a night. I've done quite enough damage for the time being."

I'm sure Bill was quite impressed with his ride-along with one of Maine's finest.

Epilogue:
The Ultimate Sacrifice

Shortly before Memorial Day of 2011, I was once again reflecting on those who sacrificed their lives while protecting and serving the public. Like all of us in law enforcement, they were well aware of the high risks involved in performing their duties, often under extreme conditions.

Sadly the Maine Warden Service has added yet another name to the list of fallen officers. Warden Pilot Daryl R. Gordon, sixty, of Eagle Lake, Maine, died on Thursday, March 24, 2011, when the plane he was piloting crashed on Clear Lake in northern Piscataquis County. This tragic incident occurred in a remote area of the state, a place where Daryl loved to spend time enjoying the beauty of God's creation and the privacy it offered. Fortunately, Daryl's faith and strong religious strength have helped his family and friends cope with the tragedy.

This particular day was like any other in the pilot's career. He left home as usual that morning after chatting with his neighbor and good friend, retired Warden Pilot Gary Dumond. As he lifted off from the ice on Eagle Lake, he buzzed over the trees surrounding the home of his minister and good friend, Pastor Gary Gardner of the Mountain View Bible Church. The pastor recalls signaling Daryl with a cordial wave of his hand as he watched him depart the countryside, on what would become the pilot's final journey to the heavens above.

Daryl piloted his plane to the Greenville headquarters that morning, where he met with fellow associates. At the plane base he swapped his aircraft for another while his received the usual maintenance inspections required to keep it airworthy. The day was as normal as any of those preceding it: The sky was clear, and the terrain below was covered with snow and ice as the spring thaw was beginning to encroach upon the North Country.

Later that afternoon, Daryl received a request to assist a fellow warden, Andrew Smart, who had mired his snow machine in the slush on Big Eagle Lake, a remote area located along the Allagash Waterway. Together they managed to free the snow machine after flying off to find a come-along to help them in their efforts. The usual chatter and camaraderie between the two wardens was like that of any other day. The young warden showed his appreciation for Daryl's help as they parted company later that afternoon. Daryl was last observed heading off into the wild blue yonder, presumably bound for home, while Andrew Smart returned to his cruiser via snowmobile. It was the last time Daryl was seen alive. There were a few scattered snow squalls in the area, but the experienced pilot wasn't worried.

Later that evening, Rita Gordon became concerned when she didn't hear from her husband as darkness settled in. She called other local wardens, inquiring whether Daryl had decided to stay at one of the many warden camps in the area due to the snow squalls that had blown through the region earlier in the day. But no one could tell her if he had in fact holed up elsewhere, waiting for the conditions to improve.

A search for Daryl began around 8 p.m. that evening and continued on through the night. Early the next morning at approximately 9 a.m., a faint signal from an aircraft emergency locator was detected by a Civil Air Patrol aircraft searching the terrain in the vicinity where Daryl was last observed. Within minutes a Maine Forestry Service helicopter and the Civil Air Patrol plane found Daryl and his crashed airplane upon the frozen lake. Whether the crash resulted from the effects of the previous day's heavy snow squall or if it was due to some other incident was yet to be determined.

In the words of the clergyman who spoke at Daryl's funeral, "God planned for his son to come home on that particular day." According to his family, Daryl was well prepared for the homecoming.

On March 30, 2011, Daryl was remembered by thousands of his devastated colleagues in a "Ceremony of Life" held at the Augusta Civic Center in Augusta, Maine. It truly was a hero's ceremony, fit for a king. There were dignitaries and colleagues from all around the country filling the packed auditorium, remembering and honoring the sacrifice of one of Maine's finest. Maine Warden Service Colonel Joel Wilkinson and his team of young wardens made me some proud of the agency I'd worked for, conducting themselves with a tremendous amount of dignity and integrity while honoring the life of their fallen hero.

Unfortunately the department had been called upon to perform the same task in the past. And like so many times before, this ceremony of life was highly emotional and extremely well-orchestrated. Daryl would've been proud, and, honestly speaking, I'm not so sure he wasn't watching the tribute from the heavens above. I was pleased to see so many old friends gathered at the solemn affair—wardens who, like myself, had served their time participating in the greatest profession on earth, all paying our final respects.

Dean Varney, the son of pilot Richard Varney, presented the Gordon family with the flag that had been placed on his own father's casket after a helicopter crash claimed the life of his dad on September 27, 1972. A solemn line of game wardens' wives slowly marched single file up to the casket as a show of respect and honor. On the way back to their seats they presented Gordon's widow, Rita, with 125 white roses representing the Maine Warden Service personnel. The hall was filled to near capacity with uniformed officers from every New England state and even the Province of Quebec, Canada.

Governor Paul LePage and his wife joined a large contingent of Maine legislators seated inside the auditorium, paying their respects. Uniformed officers from a variety of agencies— the Maine State Police, several neighboring state conservation officers, Forestry Department agents, Border Patrol Sea and Shore, the fire marshal's office, county deputies, and a host of other local law enforcement personnel—marched into the building as the State Police bagpipers played. The tunes tore at the mourners' emotions as a dull drumbeat and "Amazing Grace" echoed throughout the space. Tears flowed freely as a host of colleagues, family members, and friends offered emotional tributes to the fallen pilot.

After the celebration, we all stood silently at attention outside of the auditorium when the last call for Warden Pilot 2202 was broadcast over the State Police radio, a moving display of departmental honor. A flight of four low-flying aircraft in tight formation flew over the area as seven members of the Warden Service funeral detail fired a volley of shots, in the traditional twenty-one-gun salute. Then there was a moment of silence, followed by a lone trumpeter playing "Taps." Even the toughest of hardened officers standing in the group were moved to tears at this special tribute to their fallen comrade.

Soon afterward a contingent of approximately six hundred officers formed a funeral procession of cruisers with flashing blue lights. They headed north on I-95 to the rural country cemetery in St. Albans where Daryl's body was finally laid to rest. Flying low above the funeral entourage was a squad of department airplanes, yet another tribute to their fallen comrade.

The good Lord blessed the ceremony on this late-March day by providing a cloudless sky and warm temperatures. Two days later, we suddenly found ourselves smothered in an early-spring nor'easter with high winds and blowing snow totally encompassing the landscape. I wondered if perhaps God purposely delayed the violent weather until his son had received the official send-off he was entitled to. The entire ceremony was conducted without a hitch, almost as if Daryl was himself at the helm.

Like Warden Pilots George Townsend and Richard Varney, who had previously lost their lives, Daryl Gordon eventually had his name inscribed upon the polished granite stone at the Officers' Memorial as the fifteenth member of the Warden Service to have made the ultimate sacrifice doing what he loved best—serving the sportsmen of Maine.

Lest we forget, there are a few other members of the agency who died in plane crashes, although they were not officially on duty at the time of their deaths, and their names are not included on the granite stone. Retired Warden Pilot Jack McPhee was killed in May of 2003 when his small plane crashed as he was tracking a lynx via a radio-tracking signal. Jack served the northern region as a Warden Pilot prior to his retirement. He was a real pro at his trade, and without a doubt, he died doing what he loved most. Game warden Barry Woodard was killed in the late 1980s while a passenger in a Civil Air Patrol plane that tragically went down at the end of the runway in Augusta. Barry was only thirty-two years old at the time, and left behind his young wife and eighteen-month-old child. Although their names are not inscribed on the memorial, they are forever lodged in this writer's memory. They, too, were among the best.

I wish I could say that Daryl's tragic death will be the last, but unfortunately, I'm sure that in due time, somewhere, someplace, another officer will make the ultimate sacrifice, and we will once again gather in solemn tribute for yet another fallen brother or sister. All law enforcement personnel accept the risks inherent in our profession without hesitation, and know that a similar fate could await each and every one of us.

If you ever get to Augusta, I hope you'll pay homage at the Maine Law Enforcement Officers' Memorial, located a short distance away from our state capitol. The names inscribed upon the granite represent true heroes—folks who gave their all so the rest of us could feel safe and secure as we roam and enjoy the vast wilderness of our great state.

About the Author

John Ford Sr., a native Mainer, comes from a long line of Maine game wardens. He was sworn into the service shortly after finishing up a four-year stint in the US Air Force. He spent all of his twenty-year warden career in Waldo County in central Maine. Upon his retirement in 1990, he was elected as county sheriff, and reelected in 1994. He has written a local newspaper column, and is a regular contributor to the *Northwoods Sporting Journal*. His first book, *Suddenly, the Cider Didn't Taste So Good!* was published by Islandport Press in 2012. He is also a painter, known for his wildlife artwork, and is the guest speaker at numerous events in Maine. He lives with his wife in Brooks, Maine.

Center Point Large Print
600 Brooks Road / PO Box 1
Thorndike, ME 04986-0001 USA

(207) 568-3717

US & Canada:
1 800 929-9108
www.centerpointlargeprint.com